WITHDRAWN
UTSA LIBRARIES

D0570993

T1-AXQ-635

43.861

α3·85 Tx2

JANUA LINGUARUM

STUDIA MEMORIAE
NICOLAI VAN WIJK DEDICATA

edenda curat

C. H. VAN SCHOONEVELD

Indiana University

Series Practica, 126

STRUCTURES
OF MODIFICATION
IN CONTEMPORARY
AMERICAN ENGLISH

by

GEORGE A. HOUGH 3RD
MICHIGAN STATE UNIVERSITY

1971
MOUTON
THE HAGUE · PARIS

Copyright 1971 in The Netherlands.
Mouton & Co. N.V., Publishers, The Hague.

No part of this book may be translated or reproduced in any form, by print, photoprint, microfilm, or any other means, without written permission from the publishers.

LIBRARY OF CONGRESS CATALOG CARD NUMBER: 72—144013

PRINTED IN HUNGARY

LIBRARY
University of Texas
At San Antonio

PREFACE

This study was originally submitted to the Department of English at Michigan State University as a dissertation in partial fulfillment of requirements for the doctoral degree. In its present form, it has been modestly revised: in some instances to make for easier reading, in some instances to smooth out some of the awkwardness inherent in the dissertation format, in some instances to bring references up to date. A number of minor errors that escaped notice in the orignal manuscript have also been corrected.

The study and its findings stand as originally presented in 1965. There is no way of updating or revising an analysis of a specific sample of language. The only way of doing better or of bringing such a study up to date is to draw a new sample and begin again. If I were to undertake a similar study, I would make a few changes in detail, but the original analysis can, I think, stand on its merits.

My own interest in the structure of the English language is reflected in this analysis of structures of modification. Also reflected is my conviction, as a long-time newspaper writer and editor, that the informal and topical use of English in the newspaper offers an interesting and relatively untapped source of data about the contemporary language.

The study itself owes a great deal to previous research into various aspects of American English syntax. The extensive work of Charles Carpenter Fries, W. Nelson Francis and Eugene Nida, in particular, served as a guide throughout this study. Whatever errors there may be in this study in assumption, description, or conclusion are entirely my own.

My thanks are due to a number of persons who assisted me in a number of ways, especially Professor Russel B. Nye and Professor William W. Heist of Michigan State University who guided the writing of my dissertation and gave me valuable counsel and encouragement. I am also indebted to Professor John C. Street of the University of Wisconsin and to the late Professor Hans Wolff of Northwestern University, both of whom taught me much about the English language.

GAH 3rd

TABLE OF CONTENTS

LIST OF TABLES

I

NATURE AND SCOPE OF THE STUDY

This study is an attempt to shed some light on one type of linguistic structure, that structure which is sometimes called a structure of modification.[1] It is based on a fairly limited but statistically ample corpus of 1,200 sentences taken from four metropolitan daily newspapers for the two years 1894 and 1964. The study is purely descriptive.

From various sources a catalog of the various forms that modification may take was compiled and the sentences in the corpus were examined to see whether these structures did occur, in what ways, and how frequently. Sentences taken from the newspapers were selected as the corpus for several reasons. First, because of the writer's long association with newspapers and interest in the problems of writing newspaper copy; second, because it is a contention of the writer that the syntax of newspaper copy is distinctive and has its own style and its own idiosyncrasies; third, in the expectation that if some of the facts about newspaper syntax could be established, further studies might result and comparisons could be made with other writing styles — fiction, magazine articles, and the spoken language.

Linguists have paid very little attention to the style of newspaper writing. Newspapers are often a source of lexical items, and quite often oddities in newspaper headlines are picked up by a linguist and used as a point of departure for some point he wishes to make about language in general or some particular form.[2] However, as far as the writer has been able to determine, no studies have been made of grammar based entirely on materials taken from the newspapers.

---

[1] Charles Carpenter Fries, *The Structure of English* (New York and Burlingame, Harcourt, Brace & World, Inc., 1952, reprinted 1961), hereafter cited as *Structure*, pp. 202—239, and W. Nelson Francis, *The Structure of American English* (New York, The Ronald Press, 1958), hereafter cited as *American English*, pp. 292 and 297 *ff.*

[2] See Barbara M. H. Strang, *Modern English Structure* (New York, St. Martin's Press, 1962), hereafter cited as *Modern English*, p. 94, and Stuart Robertson, revised by Frederic G. Cassidy, *The Development of Modern English* (Englewood Cliffs, N. J., Prentice-Hall, Inc., 1954), pp. 211—212, and *Structure*, p. 62.

A. THE NEWSPAPER SAMPLE

The sample or corpus on which this study is based is drawn from four major metropolitan daily newspapers: the *New York Times*, the New York *Herald-Tribune*, the Chicago *Tribune*, and the San Francisco *Chronicle*.[3] All four are well edited newspapers with high standards. They rank well in the estimation of editors and professors of journalism, and writing in these newspapers can be considered a good standard form of informal American English.

The *Times* is frequently called the nation's leading newspaper. In a survey conducted in 1960 by Edward L. Bernays, the public relations counselor, the *Times* rated first in a list of the top ten daily papers in this country.[4] It received 91 per cent of the votes cast by the newspaper publishers who participated in the poll.

In the same poll, the *Herald-Tribune* ranked tenth and the *Tribune* and *Chronicle* were in a list of runners-up which missed the first ten places. A poll conducted by the *Saturday Review* in 1961, this time among teachers of journalism, found the *Times, Herald-Tribune*, and *Tribune* all in the first ten.[5] The *Chronicle* was in the list of runners-up. *Time* in its own list of the top ten dailies in 1964 listed the *Times* among its choices.[6] None of the other three papers used in this study were included in *Time's* list.

1. The Times

The *New York Times* was founded in 1851 by Henry J. Raymond, George Jones and Edward B. Wesley. It was a penny paper and, Frank Luther Mott considered, unusually well-edited.[7] For a generation, the *Times* was vigorous and under expert direction, but by the early 90's the paper was in difficulties. By 1896 when it was sold to Adolph S. Ochs, circulation had fallen to 9,000 and the paper was losing $ 1,000 a day. Ochs started the *Times* back on the long road which led eventually to superiority. Today the *Times* is probably the most complete newspaper published anywhere in the world and it is at

---

[3] The New York *Times* Feb. 1894 and Feb. 1964; the New York *Tribune*, Feb. 1894; the New York *Herald-Tribune*, Feb. 1964; the *Chicago Daily Tribune*, Feb. 1894, Feb. 1964; the San Francisco *Chronicle*, Feb. 1894, Feb. 1964; available on microfilm. See George A. Schwegmann, Jr., ed., *Newspapers on Microfilm* (Washington, D. C.: Library of Congress, 1963), pp. 27, 55, 134, and 137. The *Herald-Tribune* files include the files of the New York *Tribune* from 1841—1924.

[4] Anon., "The Top 10 Dailies Almost Same as in 1952 Poll", *Editor and Publisher* (April 9, 1960), 66.

[5] John R. Tebbel, "Rating The American Newspaper", *Saturday Review* (May 13, 1961), 60—64.

[6] Anon., "The Top U.S. Dailies", *Time* (Jan. 10, 1964), 58.

[7] Source of the historical data on the four newspapers is Frank Luther Mott, *American Journalism* (New York, The Macmillan Company, 1962).

least as well edited, if not better edited, than any other newspaper in the world. Circulation figures for the *Times*:[8]

	1893	*1964*
daily	45,000	603,574
Sunday		1,283,785

2. *The Herald-Tribune*

The *Herald-Tribune* is the descendent of two distinguished New York newspapers, Horace Greeley's *Tribune*, which was founded in 1841, and the *Herald*, founded in 1835 by the elder James Gordon Bennett. The *Tribune* came into the hands of Whitelaw Reid in 1873, after Greeley's death, and although still somewhat sensational, had, according to William Cullen Bryant, taken over some of the *Evening Post*'s reputation as a paper for gentlemen and scholars. It was lively, well edited, and vigorous. For a time John Hay, the biographer of Lincoln, was an assistant editorial writer for the *Tribune*. The *Tribune* acquired the *Herald* in 1924 from Frank Munsey for $5,000,000. The combination of two faltering dailies proved successful, and the *Herald-Tribune* was a close competitor of the *Times* through the 1920's and 1930's. The *Times* pulled ahead in the post-World War II period, but in the two or three years after the sale of the *Herald-Tribune* to John Hay Whitney, the paper blossomed again. It was in 1964 very carefully edited and extremely well written although nowhere near as voluminous as the *Times*. Circulation figures for the *Herald-Tribune*:

	1893	*1964*
daily	80,000	282,000
Sunday		363,384

The *Herald-Tribune* was merged with two other New York newspapers in 1965 to become the hybrid *World-Journal-Tribune*. An extended strike and staggering losses when the merged newspaper did publish culminated in suspension of the *World-Journal-Tribune* and disappearance of the last vestige of the pioneering journalism of Greeley and the Bennetts.

---

[8] Circulation for 1893 came from *The S. H. Parvin's Sons Co. Newspaper Directory 1893—94* (Cincinnati, The S. H. Parvin's Sons Co., 1893), pp. 64, 83 and 108, and for 1964 from the *Editor and Publisher International Yearbook 1964* (New York, Editor and Publisher, 1964).

3. The Tribune

The *Tribune* was founded in 1847 and struggled for survival until it was purchased in 1855 by Joseph Medill, a few years later one of the principal backers of Abraham Lincoln's candidacy. The *Tribune*, firmly managed by Medill, grew into one of the four great newspapers published in Chicago just before the turn of the century. In the mid-90's, Medill surrendered control of the paper to his son-in-law, Robert W. Patterson, and later, under the direction of Medill's grandson, Robert R. McCormick, the *Tribune* grew in circulation, power, and prestige. Calling itself modestly the World's Greatest Newspaper, the *Tribune* achieved a circulation of a million copies a day just before World War II. Since McCormick's death in 1955, the paper has been published by the Tribune Company under management of McCormick's editorial heirs. Circulation figures for the *Tribune:*

	1893	*1964*
daily	78,000	831,904
Sunday		1,138,268

4. The Chronicle

The *Chronicle* was the great West Coast newspaper of the generation after the Civil War. Founded in 1865 by two teen-age brothers, it soon became a vigorous, newsy and profitable newspaper. One of the owners, Charles De Young, was shot and killed in 1880 as a result of the paper's feud with the Workingmen's Party; his brother, M. H. De Young, supervised the paper's operations until his death in 1925. In 1964 the *Chronicle* was the only independent daily newspaper in San Francisco and its only competition comes from the Hearst papers, the morning and Sunday *Examiner* and the evening *News-Call-Bulletin*. As a result of a subsequent merger, the *Chronicle* is alone in the morning field, the *Examiner* is published in the evening and the two newspapers together produce a single Sunday paper, the *Examiner and Chronicle*. Circulation figures for the Chronicle:

	1893	*1964*
daily	61,156	330,225
Sunday		352,138

B. THE 70 YEARS FROM 1894 TO 1964

In the history of a language, 70 years is not an appreciable span of time, but in the recent history of journalism, 70 years is an age. In 1894 the Gilded Age of the Greeleys, the Bennetts, the Danas, the Medills, and the other giants of journalism was over. The Linotype had come into the composing room in

1886; engraving of photographs had begun in the early 1880's; in 1889 Hoe's sextuple press fed by three rolls of newsprint turned out 48,000 copies an hour of a twelve-page paper for the New York *Herald*. The great Joseph Pulitzer had just established himself in New York and the new *World* building was one of the sights of the city. The telephone and typewriter were new in the city room and the press associations were just beginning to pour world and national news onto the telegraph editor's desk.

Newspapers in 1894 were stepping out of their infancy into their young manhood. It was the beginning of the period of mass circulation, cheap newsprint, and yellow journalism. It was a period of growth and excitement and the daily newspaper was just on the threshold of the modern age. The newspaper was just past the crest of success won by vigorous, personal editorial direction and just poised on the threshold of the period of great mechanical progress which lasted from the late 1890's to the end of World War II.

In 1964 newspapers had reached maturity. They had achieved mass circulation and financial success thanks to the mechanical production methods available in the 1890's and since perfected, and thanks also to the great growth this nation experienced from the 1890's on. Today the neswpaper, like the rest of society, is in the early days of the nuclear and electronic age, facing new problems and great changes. The computor and the communications satellites promise to alter newspapers in the next 70 years even more than the Linotype and the web-perfecting press did in the 70 years after the 1890's.

If ever differences existed, they exist between the American newspaper of the 1890's and of the 1960's. The newspaper of today is produced differently, it is edited by a new kind of journalist, it is read by a new kind of American. Today's newspapers are as different as black is from white from the newspapers of the 1890's.

Whether there are any differences in the way news was written in the 1890's and the way it is written today — grammatical differences, that is — is one of the question this study has set out to determine. As we shall see later, some differences do exist. There is, for example, a definite trend toward a greater use of nouns as modifiers of other nouns. Examination of the summary tables in the final chapter will show in more detail the shifts in usage of the various types of modifiers over the seventy-year period under examination. Whether these shifts are part of a general shift going on throughout the language or are peculiar to newspaper writing will have to be determined by further studies.

C. METHODOLOGY

The corpus, 1,200 sentences, is a four-way sample of the writing of staff members of four American daily newspapers. The newspapers were selected because they were available in the two years 1894 and 1964 and because they

represent a good, high-quality form of journalism. All four papers had a reputation in 1894 and all had a reputation in 1964. They are all, by coincidence,
morning newspapers, and they represent the geographical differences between
East Coast, Middle West, and the Far West.[9]

The month of February was selected as the sample month as a recent
month in 1964 (the time of the writing of this book) and a period for which
microfilm copies of the 1964 newspapers were already available. The fourth
week of the month was selected with the aid of a table of random numbers
as the six-day period from which the materials of the corpus were to be drawn.
Daily issues, Monday through Saturday, were used in drawing the sample.
The issues were those of Thursday, February 22; Friday, February 23; Saturday,
February 24; Monday, February 26; Tuesday, February 27; and Thursday,
February 28 in 1894. In 1964 the issues were those of Saturday, February 22;
Monday, February 24; Tuesday, February 25; Wednesday, February 26;
Thursday, February 27; and Friday, February 28.

Sentences were drawn from locally written news stories spread as much
as possible through the entire issue of the paper. Only locally written stories
were used. No press association copy, no syndicated material, no stories written
by correspondents and originating outside the city of publication, no editorials,
no columns, and no sports or women's page stories were included. Content
or subject matter of news stories was not otherwise considered, and it is pro-
posed that these exclusions left the sample representative of general, not
specialized, newswriting.

Two sets of sentences were drawn from 75 different news stories in each
of the four newspapers for each of the two years. The first set of sentences
was the initial sentence in each news story; these sentences will be referred to
hereafter as lead sentences. From the four newspapers 300 lead sentences
were drawn, seventy-five from each paper for 1894 and the same number
from each paper in 1964, 600 lead sentences in all. The second set of sentences, another 600, represents as nearly as possible the entire news story. For
this sample, sentences were selected in rotation from the first, second, third,
and fourth quarters of the news story, the first full sentence in each quarter
being selected in each instance. These sentences will be referred to hereafter
as representative sentences.

Three comparisons are possible from this sample: (1) between newswriting
in general and the lead sentence, (2) between the four newspapers, and (3)
between writing in two different years separated by a span of seventy years.

---

[9] The four newspapers were selected on the basis of the criteria cited above. In content
analysis it is seldom the practice to draw titles on a random basis. For a discussion of
the problem of selecting titles for content analysis, see Richard W. Budd, Robert K.
Thorp and Lewis Donohew, *Content Analysis of Communications* (New York, The Macmillan Company, 1967), pp. 23—25.

Comparisons between features in the four newspapers are based on too small a sample to have much validity, but comparisons between the 300-sentence sample in the two years and between lead and representative sentences should have validity.

Sentences were drawn as much as possible from the entire newspaper. Selection was made beginning on page one and with the outside left-hand column starting at the top of the page. The first local story was chosen from the first column, and if there was no local story in the first column, then the first local story was taken from the second column. The second story selected was the first local story in the left-hand column on page two, and so on in order.

Issues of the four papers in 1894 were usually of ten or twelve pages and the sample pretty well represents something from every page. In a few instances it was necessary to start back through the paper a second time, this time taking the second local story from each page.

This was a systematic random sample rather than an unrestricted random sample. It is intended to be representative of the universe from which it was taken and to be large enough to present reasonably accurate data.[10] The 300 sentences from the two years, representing both lead sentences and representative sentences, is a large enough sample to avoid undue error, and, according to standard tables, standard error in a sample this size would be approximately 5 percentage points, plus or minus. To reduce the possibility of error by as much as 1 percentage point would require that the size of the sample be increased from 300 to 600 sentences.[11] The increase in accuracy thus achieved would hardly be worth the amount of effort involved. Altogether, the sample of 1,200 sentences ran to more than 31,000 words. The sample:

	1894	*1964*	
lead sentences	300	300	
representative sentences	300	300	
total	600	600	1,200

[10] Gustav Herdan maintains that any sample of language is random unless one just picks out the items he is looking for. See *The Calculus of Linguistic Observations* ('s-Gravenhage, Mouton & Co., 1962), p. 25, where he says that: "My contention is that the linear sequences of linguistic forms in written texts or speech are random series with respect to certain quantitative characteristics, and any sampling procedure, be it by disconnected units, or by continuous pieces of text, by pages, chapters, etc., will give a random sample of such quantitative characteristic; that is, provided it does not consist in a direct or indirect selection of categories of just such characteristics we are sampling for."

[11] See David J. Luck, Hugh G. Wales and Donald A. Taylor, *Marketing Research* (Englewood Cliffs, N. J., Prentice-Hall, Inc., 1961), p. 197.

D. STRUCTURES OF MODIFICATION

This study is an analysis of the various STRUCTURES OF MODIFICATION in a particular sample of present-day American English. Structures of modification are linguistic units consisting of at least two words, a HEAD and a MODIFIER. All structures of modification must consist of these two IMMEDIATE CONSTITUENTS. Either the head or the modifier may be a single word or a sequence of related words. The following are examples of structures of modification:

> the slithy *toves*
> *man* of letters
> deep *in the wabe*

The head, underlined, is that part of the structure of modification which can replace the whole structure in a sentence. For example, *We saw the slithy toves* could be changed to read *We saw toves*. The expendable words in the sequence *the slithy toves* are *the* and *slithy*, and these two words are, by process of elimination, modifiers. What remains, the word *toves*, is the head. Modifiers are that part of a structure of modification which cannot be substituted for the head. In the sentence below, note the identification of the head and modifier on the basis of elimination:

> We found ourselves *deep in the wabe*.
> We found ourselves *in the wabe*.

In the underlined structure of modification, *deep* can be eliminated and is, hence, the modifier, while *in the wabe* can substitute for the entire structure and is, hence, the head. The entire structure of modification consists of a head and a modifier. Note, too, that the head here is not a single word, but a sequence of three words.

This study follows Trager and Smith in defining a words as a base with or without one or more affixes and with a superfix.[12] Trager and Smith cite *taker* and *Plato* as examples of words. In the structures above, *man, toves, deep, in, the*, and *letters* are all words, to cite only a few examples. A SEQUENCE is merely a group of two or more related words organized into a meaningful entity: *old man, in the woods, down here, way off, this afternoon*. Without need for analysis, any native speaker would recognize these as meaningful. Francis terms such entities GRAMMATICAL STRUCTURES.[13] Hockett refers to them as

---

[12] George L. Trager and Henry Lee Smith, Jr., *An Outline of English Structures* (Washington, D. C., American Council of Learned Societies, 1957, fifth printing), pp. 55—57.
[13] *American English*, p. 223.

CONSTRUCTS.[14] They are sometimes called PHRASES or GROUPS, and here, following Wolff, they will be referred to as *sequences*.[15]

Single words or sequences may serve as heads in structures of modification. Modifiers may, in the same way, be single words or sequences. Heads, we will find, may be nouns, verbs, adverbs, adjectives, function words, prepositional sequences, noun sequences, clauses, verb sequences, verbs and their complements, and entire sentences. Modifiers may consist of nouns, verbs, adverbs, adjectives, function words, prepositional sequences, noun sequences, clauses, verbs and their complements, and entire sentences.

Analysis of structures of modification must depend, first of all, on identification of a given sequence as a structure of modification, and, second, on classification of the modifier and head. Sequences had, first to be classified by type: noun-headed structure of modification, adjective-headed, adverb-headed, and so on. Then the various modifiers of each class of structure had to be identified as to type: noun-modifier, adjective-modifier, and so on.

Once a sequence had been identified as a structure of modification consisting of a head and a modifier, one had only to identify the head and to assign the structure to its proper class: noun-headed structure, adjective-headed structure, and so on. Analysis of the modifier involved four points: (1) what kind of modifier, noun-modifier, adjective-modifier, prepositional-sequence-modifier, and so on; (2) what position did the modifier occupy in relation to its head; (3) with what frequency did each type of modifier appear; and (4) in some instances, did the modifier appear alone with its head or in company with other modifiers?

Position of the modifier presents little problem. If the head is a single word, the modifier will normally be either pre-posed or post-posed. Very occasionally the modifier will appear in some other position; for example, in a noun-headed structure of modification the prepositional sequence which modifies the noun-head is normally post-posed, but will sometimes appear pre-posed. If the head is a sequence instead of a single word, modifiers may be included within the sequence as, for example, an adverb-modifier which may appear either pre-posed or post-posed to a single-word verb-head, but which may also appear between a verb-head and its auxiliary.

Determining the frequency with which a given modifier appeared with a given type of head and in a given position presented no problem except that of tedium. All heads and modifiers were listed on tally sheets according to the type of head, position and type of modifier, and relation to other modifiers

<hr>

[14] Charles F. Hockett, *A Course in Modern Linguistics* (New York, The Macmillan Company, 1958), p. 164.

[15] I am indebted for this term to the late Hans Wolff who used it in his *Structural Highlights of American English*, which I was privileged to read in manuscript at the time the present study was begun.

Each tally sheet was double checked for accuracy of each item and the tally sheets were totalled. Totals from each tally sheet were carried over to summary sheets so that totals for each newspaper and each year could be obtained and the final figures transfer.ed to tables.

E. IDENTIFICATION OF HEADS AND MODIFIERS

Proper identification of heads and modifiers and of the various structures already mentioned, depended in large part on identification of the four form-class words: nouns, verbs, adjectives, and adverbs. In most instances identification was simple and obvious. In a few instances, however, ambiguity existed for one or more reasons. Sometimes the various syntactic signals were missing; sometimes the word in question had the same morphemic form as a word normally associated with another form class; sometimes the word was out of normal position; sometimes the word was a replacement for a member of another form class.

In the main, however, identification of heads or modifiers as nouns, verbs, adverbs, or adjectives was readily accomplished by simple comparison of the five signals of syntactic structure cited by Francis.[16] These are characteristic position in a sentence or sequence, inflection, regular appearance with specified function words, derivational contrast, and prosodic contrast.

1. Identification of Nouns

Most nouns were readily identified by these syntactic signalling devices, and usually more than one signal of identification was found. Many nouns, for example, will appear in characteristic position and also show noun inflection and be paired with function words associated only with nouns.[17]

Francis considers noun markers, those characteristic function words found only in association with nouns, as the most important device for identifying a word as a noun. The noun markers consist of seven groups of function words: the definite article *the;* the indefinite article *a/an;* the various personal pronouns; the specifiers *this/that* and their plural forms *these/those;* the cardinal numbers; the negative *no;* and a fairly long list of function nouns. A more complete discussion of noun markers appears in Chapter I.

Noun inflection is the second significant signal identifying nouns. Nouns show two types of inflection: first, the suffix-*'s* which indicates possession; second, the suffixes -*s* or -*es* which indicate more than one. For example:

[16] See *Structure*, pp. 65—141, and *American English*, pp. 229—290. This discussion basically follows *American English* which is somewhat more succinct than *Structure*.
[17] *American English*, pp. 237—252.

possessive inflection   boy/boy's
                                        wife/wife's
                                        man/man's

plural inflection   boy/boys
                                        wife/wives
                                        house/houses
                                        tree/trees

Irregular plurals appear fairly frequently, but their identification poses few problems. No one is likely to mistake man/men, tooth/teeth, medium/media simply because they are irregular plurals.

Derivational contrast also serves to signal that a word is a noun. Nouns derived from verbs, adjectives, other nouns, or built up from bound bases show characteristic derivational suffixes like *-age*, *-ee*, *-cy*, *-ist*, *-dom*, and *-ity*:

breakage
employee
intricacy
violinist
freedom
facility

A few noun suffixes are ambiguous, the *-ing* of *running*, *parking*, *smoking*, for example, but where there is such ambiguity other means of identification are often present.

Characteristic position also serves to identify nouns and Francis cites the chief position filled by nouns as the position immediately before a verb, that is, the subject position in a sentence with normal word order. A test frame can be constructed to determine whether a given word will fit this position and is, thus, a noun by definition:

(the) _____ leaves the depot daily
             train
             bus
             passenger
             dispatch

Finally, some nouns show prosodic contrast with identical words, that is words with the same morphemic form, which belong to another form class. For example, the words *subject*, a noun, and *subject*, a verb, which are morphemically identical, but can be differentiated because they have different stress: they contrast prosodically. For example:

The *súbject* is not to be discussed.   (noun)
I don't want to *subjéct* you to that. (verb)

A number of examples of this type of prosodic contrast between nouns and verbs can be found: *imprint, suspect, contract, object,* and others.

These various signals of syntactic structure are valid only in context, however, for the syntactic value of a given word depends on a number of simultaneous and related factors. Identifying signals valid in isolation may have no validity when actual instances of use are considered. The word *today,* for example, may be a noun in one context, but an adverb in another. The fact that *today* can be inflected for possession and the plural when it appears in subject position does not alter the fact that it cannot be so inflected when it appears in a position characteristic of adverbs.[18]

2. *Identification of Verbs*

Verbs can be readily identified in most instances by the five signals of syntactic structure already cited. Verbs have characteristic position in the sentence, they have characteristic inflection, they appear with certain readily identifiable function words, they show derivational contrast, and they show prosodic contrast.[19]

For verbs, characteristic position in the sentence is, according to Francis, between two nouns, as in the following examples from the materials examined in this study:

these men *deserve* the gratitude
the effigy *had* black-painted features

Inflection readily serves to identify verbs. Verb inflection is by means of the suffixes *-s, -ed, -en,* and *-ing,* which differentiate between present tense, past tense, past participles, and present participles:

present	*-s* in the third person singular
	tests
	results
past	*-ed* in all persons in both singular
	and plural
	filed

---

[18] There is a difference between a word's morphological class and its syntactic class; where there is a conflict, morphology accedes to syntax. Position, *i.e.,* word order, is the more significant factor. See *Structure,* p. 141.

[19] *American English,* pp. 252—268.

                                  asked
                                  aimed
                                  explained

participle   *-ed* in most verbs and *-en* in some
                                  was donated
                                  were greeted
                                  was swollen
                                  had been beaten

present participle   *-ing* in all cases
                                  is acting
                                  replacing
                                  calling

Function words are useful in identifying irregular verb forms although from a practical standpoint the irregular verbs are familiar enough to most speakers. Function words associated with verbs are the various forms of the verb *to be* and the verb *to have* and the modal auxiliaries. For example, with the function words underlined:

    was hit
    have seen
    were going

    will give
    can go

Derivational contrast provides another syntactic signal for identification of verbs, but this seldom provides the only means of identification. Derivational suffixes like *-ate*, *-ize*, *-ish*, and *-en* appear on verbs like *irrigate*, *digitize*, *extinguish*, and *broaden*.

Prosodic contrast also serves to identify verbs, but the number of verbs with forms morphemically identical with words of other form classes is small.

There is seldom a serious problem in identifying verbs when they appear in a sentence or clause in characteristic subject + verb relationship. In such instances not only position, but inflection and pairing with function words also identify the verb. However, when a verb appears in other positions identification is another matter. When verbs appear as modifiers they have no accompanying function words to serve as markers and they are frequently uninflected — as is the case of the infinitive — or they have the ambiguous suffixed *-ed* or *-ing*. In such cases other means of identification are necessary: probable relationship to a head-word, relationship to a direct object, relationship to a modifier or to some other structure.

3. *Identification of Adjectives*

Position, according to Francis, is the most useful means of identification of the adjective.[20] If a word can fit both blanks in the test frame below, it is an adjective. If the word can fit the first blank, but not the second, it is not an adjective. The test frame:

the _____ thing seems very _____

      strong   strong
      relaxed   relaxed
      interesting   interesting

Nouns, verbs, and adverbs can fill the first blank, but not the second. For example:

the _____ leader is very _____

school	*nouns*
labor	
swimming	
murdered	*verbs*
injured	
retiring	
aged	*adjectives*
charming	
wise	
then	*adverb*

In this study, this test — the ability of an adjective to pair with *very* and sometimes with *quite* — proved a useful means of differentiating between adjectives and verbs with the suffixes *-ed* and *-ing*.

In addition to the test of position, it is possible to identify adjectives by the other syntactic signals: inflection, pairing with certain function words, derivational contrast and prosodic contrast.

Adjectives are inflected for comparison by means of the suffixes *-er* and *-est*:

fine	finer	finest
sharp	sharper	sharpest
nice	nicer	nicest

Certain adjectives are compared periphrastically by means of a pre-posed *more* or *most*:

[20] *American English*, pp. 268—291.

desirable   more desirable   most desirable
recent   more recent   most recent

A few other adjectives are compared irregularly, like *good* with its comparative *better* and superlative *best*.

Adjectives are frequently derived from nouns, verbs, and bound bases by
means of derivational suffixes, many of which are exclusive to adjectives
and hence provide an easy means of identifying a word as an adjective. A
few derivational suffixes are *-y*, *-al*, *-able*, and *-ful* found affixed to adjectives
like *leafy*, *fatal*, *adaptable*, and *hopeful*. Some adjective suffixes are ambiguous, particularly the *-ed* and *-ing* of adjectives like *respected* and *interesting*.

Prosodic contrast sometimes serves to differentiate between verbs, nouns,
and adjectives. For example, contrast:

He entered the *running* race.   noun
He entered the *running* stream.   verb
He was *interesting* as usual.   adjective
He was *interesting* his students.   verb

Finally, adjectives are sometimes paired with a group of function words
which Fries and Francis refer to as QUALIFIERS.[21] Qualifiers are primarily
adverbs, but a few are marked nouns. Their use is somewhat limited in the
written language, as reference to later tables will show, but Fries and Francis
report that qualifiers are in extensive use in the spoken language. Qualifiers
include such words as *very*, *quite*, *a little*, *a lot*, *more*, *most*, and *less*.

4. Identification of Adverbs

Francis suggests that the most useful test for an adverb is that of position.[22]
Any word, according to Francis, that can appear in sentence final position
after a noun or nouns, as in the test frame below, is an adverb:

the man told (us) his story _____

hopefully
aloud
somehow
over
again
today

---

[21] Francis' list of qualifiers will be found in *American English*, p. 278; Fries lists qualifiers, his Group D function words, in *Structure*, pp. 92—94.
[22] *American English*, pp. 281—288.

This may well be, as Francis says, the primary structural criterion for adverbs, but it is not particularly helpful in analysis of structures of modification in actual sentences. As we shall see in Chapter II, the position Francis posits is far more likely to be filled by one or more prepositional sequences than by an adverb, and adverbs, it turns out, are far more likely to appear post-posed to the verb they modify, and before rather than after the noun or nouns which are objects of the verb.

Adverbs are easily recognized in most instances by their derivational suffixes, the most common of which is -ly which forms adverbs from adjectives: *visibly, remarkably, woodenly, traditionally, seriously, critically*. A few other suffixes form adverbs from nouns, verbs, adjectives and bound stems:

a-	aloud	*-wise*	lengthwise
	aboard		sidewise
-s	nights	*-wards*	backwards
	evenings		homewards

A small group of adverbs is identical with certain prepositions: *in, on, out, up, down,* and others. Another group is composed of nouns and function words combined with the noun markers *some, any, every* and *no:*

somewhere	anywhere	someplace
nowhere	everywhere	anyplace

Adverbs are also inflected like adjectives for comparison and employ the same inflectional suffixes, *-er* and *-est*. Only a few adverbs, the so-called base adverbs, are inflected in this manner. Derived adverbs are inflected periphrastically, like adjectives, with a pre-posed *more* or *most*.

hard	harder	hardest
long	longer	longest
loudly	more loudly	most loudly
openly	more openly	most openly

A few adverbs are irregular, for example, *well* with its comparative *better* and its superlative *best*.

Adverbs are also identified by their association with certain function words, qualifiers, many of which are identical with the qualifiers already identified as adjective markers:

very well	*right* past
quite easily	*still* more easily
a lot better	

Another useful test of adverb identity is the substitute group. Adverbs may be divided into three substitute groups depending on whether they may be replaced by *then*, *there*, or by *thus* or *so*:

then	today	daily	seldom
	yesterday	now	later
there	outside	ahead	indoors
	down	back	downstairs
thus/so	easily	slowly	sideways
	critically	aloud	queerly

A cataloging of the various syntactic signals by which nouns, verbs, adjectives, and adverbs may be identified is deceptive. In actual practice they serve well probably 90 per cent of the time, but in the other 10 per cent difficulties arise. Morphological signals are sometimes ambiguous, as in the case of the suffixes *-ing* and *-ed*. The syntactic signal of position is sometimes ambiguous. In the case of adjectives and adverbs, the function words that serve as markers seldom appear when they would be most helpful. The language is so flexible that almost any word or structure may show up in any position in a sentence, however unlikely the possibility might be. For example, the position between the noun marker *the* and the noun is generally described as an adjective position, but it is commonly filled by nouns, not infrequently by a verb, and on rare occasions by an adverb.

In most doubtful cases identification was possible with the aid of lists of function words, derivational suffixes, and substitute groups compiled from the sources already cited.

Nouns, verbs, adjectives, and adverbs are defined, then, as words which can be identified by the various syntactic signals just described. Function words are words which are not nouns, verbs, adjectives, or adverbs and which have a syntactic function in sequences, clauses, and sentences. Fries lists fifteen separate groups of these words.[23] For the purposes of this study the most important function words were Fries' Group A, noun markers; Group B, verb markers; Group F, prepositions; and Group J, called variously adverbs, conjunctions and includers.[24]

In conclusion, identification of form class words was dependent on test frames for position; derivational contrasts with members of other form classes; various lists of identifying function words; and, to a lesser extent, inflection.

---

[23] *Structure*, pp. 87—109.

[24] For an exhaustive list of prepositions and conjunctions, see Harold Whitehall, *Structural Essentials of English* (New York and Burlingame, Harcourt, Brace & World, Inc., 1956, reprinted 1961), pp. 62—63, and pp. 72—73.

Prosodic contrast seldom was of any assistance. Occasionally substitute groups provided some assistance. Where no other criteria would do, it was found useful to compare the word or structure in question with the catalog of possible structures of modification in Nida and Francis.[25]

Form class words, as this study will show, are not the only heads, nor the only modifiers, in structures of modification. Sentences, clauses, absolute constructions, prepositional sequences, and noun-headed structures of modification appear both as heads and as modifiers. The nature of these various structures and the criteria for identifying them will be discussed in later chapters where these structures first appear.

F. LIMITATIONS OF THE STUDY

This study is not intended as a net to dredge up every possible occurrence of a particular type of head or modifier, nor as an inventory of all the heads and modifiers in the language. Nida has in his Synopsis what may well be an all-inclusive inventory of the possible types of modifiers, and he includes a substantial number of examples. The question this study seeks to answer is not what is possible, but what actually occurs in a given sample of the language.

Use of the various structures of modification is, basically, a matter of stylistics, of choice.[26] Given a wide range of possible structures to choose from, which will a speaker or writer use, how often will he use certain structures, and in what environments?

The writer has no hypothesis to prove. This study is based on the notion that language is analyzable and that any sample of language may have its own characteristics as well as the broader characteristics, or grammar, of the language of which it is a part. The characteristics of newspaper syntax, at least as far as modification is concerned, will be set forth in the pages that follow. Whether this particular sample of newspaper writing has idiosyncrasies of its own, and whether it differs from other types of writing, must depend on further comparisons.

[25] *American English*, pp. 229—290, and Eugene A. Nida, *A Synopsis of Modern English* (Norman, Okla., Summer School of Linguistics, 2d. ed., 1962), hereafter cited as *Synopsis*. Nida's most useful study was republished in a slightly revised edition by Mouton & Co. in 1966. Order of presentation of material in the 1966 revision differs slightly from the 1962 edition cited in this study.

[26] A. A. Hill defines stylistics as "all those relations among linguistic entities which are statable, or may be statable, in terms of wider spans than those which fall within the limits of the sentence". And he further defines style as "all choices of equivalent items which the language offers the user in each linguistic situation". See A. A. Hill, *Introduction to Linguistic Structures* (New York, Harcourt, Brace and Company, 1958), p. 406.

II

NOUN-HEADED STRUCTURES OF MODIFICATION: PRE-NOMINAL MODIFIERS

In a structure of modification in which the head is a noun, modifiers may appear before the noun-head or after the noun-head. Nouns appearing before the noun-head may be said to be pre-posed or in pre-nominal position, and those appearing after the noun-head may be said to be post-posed or in post-nominal position.

A. THE PRE-NOMINAL POSITION

The pre-nominal position is the position described by Fries as the characteristic position of his Class 3 words, in this study to be referred to as adjectives, which appear between the noun determiner *the* and the Form Class 1 word, a noun, indicated in the test frame below:[1]

> D   3   1   2   3
> (The) good _____ is/was good.

Nida says that attributives to the subject-head, that is, modifiers of the noun-head, precede the subject-head.[2] He presents examples like the following (modifiers underlined):

> the *good* man
> the *poor* woman

This is the position also identified by Francis as one of the characteristic adjective positions in his test frame.[3] The pre-nominal modifier appears in the position occupied by the blank in the test frame between the determiner

---

[1] *Structure*, p. 82.
[2] *Synopsis*, p. 58.
[3] *American English*, p. 268.

the and the noun, here the word *man*. The second blank represents another adjective position of no moment here.

        the _____ man seems very _____

Francis and Fries both refer to this pre-nominal position as an adjective position and Nida refers to it as an attributive position. In this study this position, between the determiner and a noun, will be considered an unrestricted modifying position and it will be seen that in addition to adjectives various form-class words and sequences can appear in this position. The test frame is:

        D   modifier   head
        (the) _____ + NOUN

This test frame represents a structure of modification whose constituents are a noun-head and a modifier or modifiers. The modifiers identified in this study as being usual modifiers of nouns include adjectives, nouns, verbs, adverbs, various determiners, and other structures including noun-headed structures of modification and structures of coordination.

No attempt will be made in this study to examine the meaning of the various modifiers or the manner in which they modify the meaning of their heads. The task here is only to identify the various modifiers and to note their distribution and frequency.

As a first step in this analysis, every noun in the corpus of 1,200 sentences was identified as a noun on the basis of one or more of the syntactic signals described previously. Noun-headed structures of modification were listed separately from nouns appearing with no modification other than the various noun markers. In the noun-headed structures of modification the noun-heads were identified on the basis of the substitution test.

Nouns fell into several distinct groups: (1) nouns unmodified except for the various noun markers; (2) nouns with a zero marker; (3) nouns with modifiers as heads of structures of modification; (4) nouns with post-nominal modifiers; and (5) nouns with both pre-nominal and post-nominal modifiers.

The types of modifiers found in pre-nominal position with noun-headed structures of modification are shown in Table 1.

TABLE 1

Distribution of modifiers in pre-nominal position in noun-headed structures of modification in lead sentences and representative sentences in all newspapers in 1894 and 1964

Modifiers	Complete Stories				Leads Only			
	1894		1964		1894		1964	
	No.	%	No.	%	No.	%	No.	%
Nouns	520	54.8	715	56.0	738	52.3	888	54.9
Adjectives	383	40.4	439	34.4	557	39.5	573	35.4
Adverbs	2	.1	2	.1	2	.1	2	.1
Verbs	15	1.6	19	1.6	15	1.1	30	1.9
total	920	96.9	1175	92.1	1312	93.0	1493	92.3
Sequences	29	3.1	101	7.9	99	7.0	124	7.7
total	949	100.0	1276	100.0	1411	100.0	1617	100.0

B. ADJECTIVES AS MODIFIERS

Adjectives represent from 35 to 40 per cent of the modifiers appearing in the pre-nominal modifying position in noun-headed structures of modification, as we can see from Table 1. Examples of adjective modifiers as given in Francis, Fries, and in Nida, include:[4]

Francis	strong
	interesting
	relaxed
Nida	good
	rich
	holy
Fries	empty
	large
	foreign

In the newspapers examined in this study, typical examples of adjectives as modifiers included:

| *Times* | current |
| | new |

[4] *American English*, p. 268; *Structure*, p. 82; *Synopsis*, p. 60.

	criminal
	broad
Herald-Tribune	sexual
	old
	explosive
	general
Tribune	main
	last
	substantial
	northern
Chronicle	initial
	usual
	own

These modifiers (in italics in the examples below) appeared in such noun-headed structures of modification as:

criminal charges	its *current* showing
general counsel	no *new* experience
broad fields	
last year	a *special* meeting

C. NOUNS AS MODIFIERS

As Table 1 shows, nouns make up somewhat more than 50 per cent of the modifiers appearing in pre-nominal position in noun-headed structures of modification. These nouns fall into three distinct groups: (1) noun adjuncts; (2) nouns with the possessive suffix-'*s;* and (3) appositives.[5] Table 2 shows the distribution of these three types of modifiers in the materials examined in this study.

1. Noun Adjuncts

Noun adjuncts are base nouns and nouns with the plural suffix -*s/es*. They represent transforms of post-nominal structures of modification like the following:

a doctor *who is a woman*	a *woman* doctor
plans *for war*	*war* plans
laws *regulating elections*	*election* laws
a meeting *set for Tuesday*	a *Tuesday* meeting

[5] *American English*, p. 299.

TABLE 2

Various types of nouns appearing in pre-nominal modifying position in noun-headed structures of modification in all newspapers in 1894 and 1964

Modifiers	Complete Stories				Leads Only			
	1894		1964		1894		1964	
	No.	%	No.	%	No.	%	No.	%
Noun Adjuncts	257	49.4	464	64.9	438	59.3	591	66.6
*Other Adjuncts	9	1.7	13	1.8	6	.9	14	1.5
total	266	51.1	477	66.7	444	60.2	605	68.1
Possessives	13	2.5	37	5.2	26	3.5	54	6.1
total	279	53.7	514	71.9	470	63.7	659	74.2
Appositives								
titles	120	23.1	77	10.8	101	13.7	58	6.5
names	118	22.7	120	16.8	155	21.0	169	19.0
other	3	.6	4	.5	12	1.6	2	.3
total	241	46.3	201	28.1	268	36.3	229	25.8
total	520	100.0	715	100.0	738	100.0	888	100.0

* Function nouns.

As Table 2 shows, this is a common pattern in newspaper stories and in the newspapers examined in this study the use of noun adjuncts as modifiers of noun-heads increased substantially between 1894 and 1964. Examples of this type of modification from Francis, Nida, and Fries, include:[6]

Francis	a *father* image
	the *day* shift
	the *women* doctors
Nida	a *steel* weld
	the *silk* hat
	a *customs* official
Fries	a *paper* knife
	an *eye* shade
	a *student* advisor

In the newspapers examined in this study the following examples are representative of noun adjuncts:

[6]*Synopsis*, p. 62; *American English*, p. 299; *Structure*, p. 210.

Tribune	*city* hall
	bomb threats
	guest speakers
Times	the *water* shortage
	faculty members
	the *election* trials
Herald-Tribune	*color* television
	two *grain* elevators
	the *city* banks
Chronicle	the *state* council
	the *insolvency* act

2. Nouns with Possessive Suffix -'s

Distinct from noun adjuncts are the nouns in pre-nominal position in structures of modification which have the possessive suffix -'s. These nouns represent transforms of post-nominal structures of modification. For example:

a doctor *who treats women*	a *women*'s doctor
a candidate *of the people*	a *people*'s candidate
a book *that belongs to John*	*John*'s book

Hill cites structures of modification like *John's book* and *the people's candidate* as characteristic of the system of modification in English.[7]

Examples of this type of pre-nominal modification taken from Francis, Nida and Fries, include:[8]

Francis	*child's* play
	a *dog's* life
	a *day's* work
Nida	a *man's* affair
	a *people's* man
	a *children's* language
Fries	a *lady's* handkerchief
	his *mother's* support
	my *father's* house

---

[7] Hill, *Linguistic Structures*, p. 142.
[8] *American English*, p. 299; *Structure*, p. 210; *Synopsis*, p. 63.

In the newspapers examined for this study, the following examples are representative of nouns with the possessive suffix -'s as modifiers:

Tribune	a *master's* degree
	the *doctor's* bookkeeper
	the *world's* production
Times	the *society's* rooms
	today's market
	the *earth's* atmosphere
	men's fertility
Herald-Tribune	four *week's* illness
	the *Lord's* prayer
	the *city's* department
	the *Yankee's* loss
Chronicle	*Boy's* Brigade
	the *Lord's* task
	Gray's harbor

3. Names as Modifiers

Neither Francis nor Nida makes any special mention of names, geographical, personal, or names of things, although Nida lists several as examples of noun adjuncts:[9]

the *Shaw* plays
the *Roosevelt* backer
a *Boston* tea-party

In this study, names of persons, geographical names, names of animate and inanimate things traditionally considered proper nouns and usually capitalized will not be differentiated from other nouns.[10] It should be noted that proper nouns make up a very large number of all nouns appearing as modifiers in pre-nominal position in noun-headed structures of modification. Some examples:

Tribune	*Chicago* stadium
	May street
	Riverdale section

[9] *Synopsis*, p. 62.
[10] For a further discussion of names as nouns, see Ralph B. Long, "The Grammar of English Proper Names", *Names* XVII (June, 1969), 109.

Times	*Brooklyn* project
	Steinway hall
	Wooster street
Herald-Tribune	*Monmouth* Park
	Syracuse University
	Chickering Hall
Chronicle	*Market* Street
	Missouri River

Several examples of names as noun-modifiers are included in the list of possessive modifiers on page 35.

4. Appositives

So far we have identified two noun-headed structures of modification: one in which the modifier is an adjective, and one in which the modifier is a noun. Where the modifier is a noun, the noun may be either a noun adjunct or a noun with the possessive suffix -'s.

With either adjective-modifiers or noun-modifiers, the modifier is readily distinguished from its noun-head on the basis of substitution. The noun-head can, in a test sentence, be substituted for the entire structure of modification which it heads. The modifier cannot substitute for the entire structure of which it is a part.

For example, in the following noun-headed structure of modification, *the war party*, the noun-modifier and the noun-head are readily distinguished by substitution:

The *war party* elected all its candidates.
The *party* elected all its candidates.

The modifier *war* is not an acceptable substitute for the noun-headed structure of modification *the war party*. A sentence, *the war elected its candidates*, would not be readily accepted as meaningful.

A somewhat different situation presents itself, however, when one of the nouns is head and the other is an appositive, for in this type of structure of modification both the noun-head and the other noun, the appositive, may freely substitute for the entire structure of modification.

Francis and Nida cite the following examples of this type of structure:[11]

---

[11] *American English*, p. 301; *Synopsis*, p. 101.

Francis   the poet Chaucer
               the disease poliomyelitis
               the product cellophane

Nida   the steamer America
               the word aesthetic

In this type of structure either noun may substitute for the entire structure because, as Fries points out, they have the same referent.[12] In the first example, *the poet Chaucer*, both *the poet* and *Chaucer* are the same person. Either *the poet* or *Chaucer* may be substituted for the entire structure of modification:

> *The poet Chaucer* wrote "The Canterbury Tales".
> *The poet* wrote "The Canterbury Tales".
> *Chaucer* wrote "The Canterbury Tales".

Another way of showing that the appositive and the noun-head have the same referent is to show that the same pronoun may be used as a substitute for both nouns:

> the poet/he
> Chaucer/he

The two pronouns fall together when we substitute the pronouns for the appositive and its noun-head. There is no loss of meaning and no necessity for making any other changes in the test sentence:

> *He* wrote "The Canterbury Tales".

There is a clear difference between the relationship of noun-appositive and its head and noun-adjunct and its head. For example, in the noun-headed structure of modification *the aircraft carrier*, the noun *aircraft* is an adjunct, not an appositive. The adjunct *aircraft* and the noun-head *carrier* are obviously not the same thing. An aircraft is a plane and a carrier is a ship. This structure, *an aircraft carrier*, fails the substitution test, too, for only *carrier*, the noun-head, will fit the blank in the test frame:

> (the) _____ is a big ship
>   carrier

Aircraft a noun-adjunct and modifier, fails to make sense in the test frame. Another appositive, *the steamer America*, however, demonstrates the equality of appositive and head. Either *steamer* or *America* will fit a test frame:

[12] *Structure*, p. 195.

(the) _____ is a ship
    steamer
    America

The appositive thus provides us with a third type of noun to fill the pre-nominal modifying position between determiner and noun-head in a structure of modification:

(the) _____ + NOUN

adjunct   the *election* fraud
                   our *war* plans
                   color television

possessive   my *father's* house
                   a *day's* journey
                   week's end

appositive   the *steamer* America
                   the *word* ism
                   my *sister* Eileen

Table 2 shows the breakdown of these three types of noun-modifiers of noun-headwords. In 1964 in both representative sentences and lead sentences adjuncts made up more than 70 per cent of the noun-modifiers. Possessive nouns account for some 5 to 6 per cent, and appositives of various types somewhere between 25 and 30 per cent.

Examples of appositives from the newspaper materials examined for this study include:

Tribune   the *Battleship* Illinois
                   the *planets* Venus and Jupiter
Times   the *Prince* Stigliani
                   the *Hotel* deLagerot
Herald-Tribune   the *Hotel* Savoy
                   a *hero* policeman
Chronicle   the *tug* Relief
                   the *steamer* Panama
                   the *tug* Fearless

This is not a common pattern in newspaper stories, as Table 2 indicates. More common are the structures in which the appositive is a name or a title:[13]

---

[13] *Synopsis*, p. 100.

Henry Smith
Walter Main

Governor Rockefeller
Mayor Wagner

These structures meet our test for the appositive. The first noun, the appositive, and the second, the noun-head, have the same referent; either appositive or noun-head may replace the entire structure of modification in a test
sentence:

> *Mayor Wagner* is a public official.
> *Wagner* is a public official.
> *The mayor* is a public official.

Nida and Francis cite these examples of title + name appositives:[14]

Nida	Professor Johnson
	Saints Peter and Paul
Francis	Professor Jones
	Vice-President Johnson

Neither Nida nor Francis mentions name + name structures in their
discussion of appositives, but Miss Strang and Curme each cite one example:[15]

| Strang | Jane King |
| Curme | John Smith |

Names make up a class of nouns which do not have pre-posed markers
except in such sentences as *He is the Professor Jones* where particular stress
is laid on specificity of the marker. This incompatability of names and markers
extends to sequences consisting of a title + name. However, when the title
— an appositive — replaces the name — the head — it requires a marker
in most instances:

Governor Rockefeller	the Governor
Mayor Wagner	the Mayor
Judge Smith	the Judge

In direct address, of course, the title does not require a marker:

Doctor, may I ask a question?

---

[14] *American English*, p. 302; *Synopsis*, p. 101.
[15] See *Modern English*, p. 82, and George O. Curme, *A. Grammar of the English Language: Vol. III Syntax* (New York, D. C. Heath, 1931), pp. 91—92.

Names in appositive structures are probably more common in newspaper stories than in any other type of written English, although as far as the writer knows there are no figures available to confirm this. Table 2 shows that names and their appositives make up somewhere around 40 per cent of all noun $+$ noun structures of modification. Examples of titles as appositive-modifiers in the materials examined in this study:

Tribune	Alderman Noble
	Lieut. Commander Schaffner
	President Wilson
Times	Governor Rockefeller
	Mayor Wagner
	Saint Paul
Herald-Tribune	Judge Burnett
	Princess Ann-Marie
	Captain Sinclair
Chronicle	Saint David
	President Kennedy
	Dr. Long
	Judge Henshaw

Examples of names as appositive-modifiers in the materials examined in this study:

Tribune	William Rummel
	D. F. Garrett
	Charles H. Percy
Times	Keith Waterhouse
	Saul Levy
	Emil Clemens
Herald-Tribune	Meade Johnson
	George W. Carr
	John Reisenweber
Chronicle	Edward Mulvey
	C. C. Morris

Newspapers insist on complete identification and prefer that wherever possible first name and middle initial be used. However, there are a number of instances of different usage.[16]

[16] For an authoritative statement on this journalistic usage, see Robert E. Garst, ed., *Style Book of the New York Times* ((New York, The New York Times Company, 1956), pp. 2—3. See also Roy H. Copperud, *Words on Paper* (New York, Hawthorn Books, Inc., 1960), pp. 100—105.

first name and middle initial (standard)
George W. Carr
John F. Kennedy

first initial and middle name
T. John Lesinski

two initials
C. C. Morris
D. F. Garrett

For the sake of simplicity, all these forms consisting of first names and initials will be considered as belonging to a single class: FIRST NAMES.

One difficulty arises, however, in assigning appositives as we have defined them, to a class of structures whose other members consist of a modifier + head. Although we have carefully avoided any discussion of the meaning of the relationship between head-word and modifier, it is perfectly clear that by the very nature of the structure of modification the modifier plays a secondary role. In appositives this is not so, for in appositives both nouns are equal. Both have the same referent, both can replace the entire structure of which they are a part. If the two nouns are equal, which is head (superior) and which modifier (subordinate)?

Decision to refer to the second noun as head and the first as the appositive-modifier may seem somewhat arbitrary, but actually it is not. First of all, in newspaper usage, the second noun is more likely to be used as a replacement for the entire structure, a fact which gives it some color of superiority, and, in the second place, there is a contrast between the appositives we have already examined and another type of appositive which will be examined when we take up post-nominal modifiers.

First reference in newspaper stories requires complete identification, structures of modification consisting of appositive + noun: name + name, title + name, title + name + name:

John C. Smith
President Johnson
Governor George Romney

In second and later references, the second noun is more likely to be employed as a replacement for the structure of modification than is the first:

John C. Smith	Smith
President Johnson	Johnson
Governor George Romney	Romney

Even where the second reference **is** itself a structure of modification, the head is most likely to be the head of the first structure:

President Johnson   Mr. Johnson

In a typical newspaper story of approximately 800 words, for example, first references included:[17]

Eugene F. (Stormy) McDonald III
Miss Joyce E. Shank
Dr. Joseph Beeman
Mrs. Susan Tanner
John B. Haeberline

Subsequent references were McDonald, 17; Miss Shank, 4; Mrs. Tanner, 2; Dr. Beeman, 1; and Haeberline, 1. Appositives which are first names are never used as replacements for the noun-head in structures of modification consisting of a first name + last name except in references to young children or to persons well known and popular where familiarity is desired:

Christopher Robin   Christopher
Soapy Williams   Soapy

Where the appositive is a title, it is frequently used in a second and later references to replace the noun-head:

President Johnson   the President
Governor Romney   the Governor
Mayor Wagner   the Mayor

Another reason for considering the second noun in these appositive structures to be the head is the contrast between structures like these:

(a) Mayor Wagner
    Judge Thompson
    Senator McNamara

(b) Wagner, the mayor, who said . . .
    Thompson, the judge, said he would . . .
    McNamara, a senator, was arrested . . .

[17] Chicago *Tribune*, Friday, Feb. 12, 1965, p. 1. col. 5.

There is contrast, too, between appositives like *the poet Chaucer* and *Chaucer the poet:*

    (a) the writer Conrad
        the boy Lincoln
        the rat Grip

    (b) Conrad the writer
        Lincoln the boy
        Grip the Rat

There is also contrast between the following structures in which the first set consists of adjective-modifier + noun-head and the second of noun-head + noun-appositive modifier:

    (a) the eighth Henry
        the great Alfred
        the younger Dumas

    (b) Henry the Eighth
        Alfred the Great
        Dumas the younger

A number of linguists consider that stress in structures like *election fraud*, an adjunct + head-noun, and *the steamer America*, an appositive + head-noun, is the same, and that both show secondary + primary stress:[18]

    elèction fráud
    the stèamer América

We have, then, two types of appositives: pre-posed to the noun-head and post-posed to the noun-head:

    Group 1 (pre-nominal) (appositive + head)

        (the) NOUN + NOUN

                the steamer America
                President Johnson
                Mr. Smith
                the writer Conrad

    Group 2 (post-nominal) (head + appositive)

[18] See Einar Haugen, "On Reading the Close Appositive", *American Speech* XXVIII (1953), pp. 165—170; and Hill, *Linguistic Structures*, p. 179.

(the) NOUN + (the) NOUN

the attorney, Smith,
the baker, Johnson,
Smith, the Democratic candidate,
Conrad the writer
Grip the Rat

D. VERBS AS MODIFIERS

Verbs are relatively infrequent as pre-nominal modifiers, and since the verbs employed as modifiers of nouns are indistinguishable from adjectives on the basis of derivational suffixes, they are frequently mistaken for adjectives. However, on the basis of the test frame suggested by Francis, one can readily differentiate adjectives and verbs with the suffixes -*ing* and -*ed*:[19]

(the) _____ NOUN is very _____

Adjectives like *interesting, convincing, loving*, or *worried, determined, confused* fit both blanks in the test frame. Verbs like *pursuing, visiting, closing* and *written, alleged*, and *strayed* will fit only the first blank in the test frame. Francis and Nida cite the following examples of verbs as pre-nominal modifiers in noun-headed structures of modification:[20]

Francis   *racing* yacht
             trotting horse
             rotting table

Nida   *floating* stick
             following example
             investigating committee
             paid bill
             written apology
             reserved section

Examples of verbs as pre-nominal modifiers in the materials examined for this study include:

Tribune   *assessed* valuation
                             pursuing detectives

[19] *American English*, pp. 303—304.
[20] *American English*, pp. 303—304; *Synopsis*, pp. 65—68.

Times	*alleged* members
	preceding week
	consulting pediatrician
	corresponding week
Herald-Tribune	*written* instrument
	marked men
	strayed sheep
	alleged hit and run
Chronicle	*Harmonized* Melodies
	Receiving Hospital

As Table 1 shows, verbs form less than 2 per cent of the modifiers of noun-heads in noun-headed structures of modification. This is a somewhat lower figure than Francis found in a count of noun-modifiers in two magazine pieces.[21]

E. ADVERBS AS MODIFIERS

There is some disagreement as to whether adverbs do appear in the pre-nominal modifying position. Nida cites examples, Fries does not mention such a possibility, and Francis states flatly that adverbs always come immediately after the noun-head.[22]

Nida cites as examples:

the *above* statement
the *outside* job
the *down* stroke

The present study indicates that while adverbs are relatively rare as pre-nominal modifiers, they do appear occasionally. For example:

an *upstairs* hideaway

More common than this kind of modification, however, is the regular use of an adverb as modifier of a function noun:

[21] Francis was apparently counting both pre-posed and post-posed modifiers. He says: "In a count of 816 noun-modifiers in two pieces in the February, 1955, issue of Harper's Magazine, one an article and the other a short story involving considerable dialogue, adjectives made up about 71 per cent of the total. The other figures were: Nouns, 20 per cent; Verbs, 7½ per cent; Adverbs, 1½ per cent. There were about twice as many noun-determiners (1,551) as there were noun modifiers." *American English*, p. 298, footnote.

[22] *American English*, pp. 304—5; *Synopsis*, pp. 64—65.

    absolutely nothing
    nearly 90

Function nouns are a special and limited list of words which frequently take characteristic noun positions in sequences or sentences, but which have other functions, and in many cases lack some or all of the morphological characteristics of nouns. Many are also noun markers: *all, any, both, his, my, this/these, that/those, few, either, each, another*, the cardinal numbers, and a few others.[23]

F. NUMBERS AS MODIFIERS

Numbers seldom get extensive treatment in studies of syntax, usually being listed as noun markers and then abandoned. However, in a discussion of the syntax of written English as it is used in newspaper stories, numbers are of some importance. They have several functions, and while not as numerous as, say, adjectives, they are interesting because of their flexibility.

Numbers appear, first of all, as noun markers in sentences like:

    One day is all he asked for.
    His report listed *10* discrepancies.

Numbers also appear as modifiers in pre-nominal modifying position in noun-headed structures of modification where they appear between a determiner and the noun-head:

    That's the *one* thing I wanted for Christmas.
    The *11* days preceding the election were busy.

Nida cites examples of numbers in this modifying position, but he lumps them with what he calls limitation adjectives: *many, most, such, last, former*.[24] He includes in this category both cardinal numbers like *one, two, three, four*, and the ordinal numbers, *first, sevond, third, fourth*, and so on. This classification ignores some of the functions of numbers and the different distribution of cardinal and ordinal numbers. In the present study cardinal numbers will be treated separately from the ordinal numbers on the basis of distribution and the derivational contrast between the suffixes *-th, -rd, -nd*, and *-st* of the ordinal numbers which contrast with the zero suffix of cardinal numbers.

---

[23] *American English*, pp. 246—249.
[24] *Synopsis*, pp. 61—62.

Ordinal numbers appear much less frequently than the cardinal numbers, and since their distribution is that of adjectives they will be regarded as adjectives in this study. Examples of ordinal numbers as noun-modifiers:

> on *third* base
> the *tenth* month

Ordinal numbers, of course, may appear in noun positions as nouns, but they do so on the same basis as other adjectives:

> He is *the best*.
> He is *the third*.

Cardinal numbers regularly appear in three positions: in noun-marker position ahead of all other modifiers of the noun-head, in modifier position between a noun marker and the noun-head, and in noun positions with or without markers and other modifiers.

As a noun marker:

> *10* days
> *10,000* dollars (written, however, as $10,000)
> *1125* Grand River

As noun modifier:

> the *six* presidents
> his *five* indictments

As a function noun in characteristic noun positions:

> They came here in *1964*.   (in prepositional sequence)
> He asked for *one*.   (in prepositional sequence)
> *Two* will be enough.   (in subject position)
> He gave me *two*.   (in object position)

Examples of the use of numbers in the materials examined in this study include:

> *Tribune*   the *1964–65* agenda
>   any *one* country
>
> *Times*   the *1948–49* season
>   the *five* contenders
>   the *ten* employes

> *Tribune*   over *200* tons
>   the *two* men

Numbers are counted as noun markers and their frequency and distribution is shown in Tables 4 and 5. When numbers appear in noun position or in modifying position between a noun marker and noun-head they are considered function nouns and included in totals of function nouns in the various tables where function nouns are shown separately.

G. SEQUENCES AS MODIFIERS

Noun-headed structures of modification may have as modifiers, as we have already seen, single words of various classes: nouns, verbs, adjectives, and adverbs. They may also have as modifiers more complex structures.[25] For example:

> (the) _____ + NOUN
>   machine shop
>   army engineers
>   school board
>   election laws
>   guided missile

Examples of this type of noun-headed structure of modification, taken from materials under examination, include:

> *Tribune*   (collective *bargaining*) *memorandum*
>   (political *science*) *department*
>   (school *board*) *nominations*
>   (welfare *department*) *trainees*
>   (Dr. *Clark's*) *music*
>   (George *Williams*) *College*
>
> *Times*   (manual *training*) *school*
>   (last *week's*) *market*
>   (machine *shop*) *skills*

---

[25] Francis treats only simpler structures of modification, but says, p. 297, that "Both the head and the modifier which are the immediate constituents of a structure of modification may themselves be structures of more or less complexity." Nida gives examples of more complex modifiers, *Synopsis*, pp. 69—88, but his examples are mostly of modifiers with their own modifiers. He cites only one example of a complex head, a coordinate sequence like *the man and his wife*.

> (woman *suffrage*) *convention*
> (Brooks *Atkinson*) *theater*

Herald-Tribune
> (supreme *court*) *decision*
> (Justice *Culler's*) *opinion*
> (Sheriff *Clancy's*) *death*

Chronicle
> (electric *fountain*) *display*
> (Main *Street*) *wharf*
> (Beale *Street*) *bankers*
> (H. K. *Byer's*) *death*

In the examples above, the noun-heads are in italics and the modifying structure of modification is enclosed in parentheses.

TABLE 3

Distribution of modifiers of noun-heads and sequence-heads by type in all newspapers in 1894 and 1964

	Complete Stories				Leads Only			
	1894		1964		1894		1964	
	No.	%	No.	%	No.	%	No.	%
Noun Head								
Single word	575	75.6	589	66.2	761	70.5	708	63.4
Sequence	30	4.0	42	4.7	89	8.2	63	5.6
Miscellaneous	29	3.6	59	6.6	59	5.5	93	8.3
total	635	83.2	690	77.6	909	84.2	864	77.4
Sequence Head*								
Single word	106	13.9	147	16.5	137	12.7	171	15.3
Sequence	10	1.4	24	2.7	19	1.8	31	2.7
Miscellaneous	12	1.9	28	3.1	15	1.4	50	4.5
total	128	16.8	199	22.3	171	15.8	252	22.6
total	763	100.0	889	99.9	1080	100.0	1116	100.0

* Noun-headed structures of modification as head in a structure of modification.

The modifying structure of modification may itself be modified, adding a layer to the structure and making it slightly more complex. For example:

Long Island university *students*
acting Queen's County *judge*
emergency stomach ulcer *operation*
railroad work rules *controversy*
American Newspaper Publishers *Association*

estimated 1,000 Southwestern Cook County *Republicans*
Illinois Fair Employment Practices *Commission*
Chicago blood donor *service*

In some instances the modifying structures of modification have post-posed rather than pre-posed modifiers:

April 14 *balloting*
attorney-general's *office*
last night's Friends of Live Music *program*
less than happy *outcome*

In some instances the head is modified by a series of structures of modification, some of them modified:

4-story, high stoop, brown-stone *dwelling*
second annual, 25-mile *handicap*
the city's 5,000 owner-driver *cabbies*

Other syntactic structures may also serve as modifiers.[26] However, in the materials under examination here the only other type of structure appearing was the coordinate sequence.[27] Some examples:

May and December *wheat*
gay and social *element*
TV and radio *stations*
news and book *dealers*
New York Geneological and Biographical *Society*
Community and Social Agency *employes*

---

[26] The sample of American English under examination here is apparently too small to include examples of all possible types of modification. Since the study was completed, however, the author has found numerous examples of prepositional sequences, subject + predicate sequences, verb + complement sequences serving as pre-posed modifiers of noun-headed structures of modification. For example:

  prepositional sequence
        an in-depth *study*
  subject + predicate sequence
        the "I hate the world, but gotta get up and face it" *type*
  verb + complement sequence
        the Save-the-Met *campaign*

[27] Francis defines a coordinate sequence, which he terms a structure of modification, as consisting of two or more syntactically equivalent units joined in a structure that functions as a single unit. See *American English*, p. 355.

Occasionally the modifying sequence will consist not of a syntactic structure, but merely of a sequence of unmodified single words:

> great, big fat *blank*

As can be seen from Table 3, sequences represent a small percentage of all modifiers of noun-headed structures of modification.

H. SEQUENCES AS HEADS

Noun-headed structures of modification consisting of a modifier and a noun-head may themselves be modified. In such cases the head is a noun-headed structure of modification and the modifiers include the same modifiers that appear in noun-headed structures of modification. Modifiers fill the position between the determiner and the head in the following test frame:

head

(the) _____ NOUN + NOUN

In the following examples, taken from the materials under examination, the head is underlined:

Tribune	oldest *past potentate*
	rare *public appearance*
	city *election board*
	West *59th Street*
	Miss *Eva Clark*
	Dr. *Aver Friedman*
	the three *area leaders*
Times	municipal *nursing school*
	different *political faith*
	nationally-known *classics scholar*
	Chinatown *apartment house*
	Philadelphia *luggage salesman*
	Gov. *John B. Connally*
	Judge *J. Wolfe Chasson*
Herald-Tribune	first *half century*
	various *election districts*
	automotive *production facilities*
	East *79th Street*

	Col. *Edmund Glenn*
	Undersheriff *John B. Sexton*
Chronicle	official *opening days*
	old *Pythian Hall*
	state *Horticultural Society*

Modifiers of noun-headed structures of modification may also consist of noun-headed structures of modification. For example:

Tribune	citizen band *radio operation*
	north side *burglary detail*
	police superintendent *O. W. Wilson*
Times	North Avenue *elevated train*
	district attorney *Frank D. O'Connor*
	Young Men's *Christian Association*
Herald-Tribune	Grace Metallious' *last piece*
	former President *Herbert Hoover*
	Number 264 *Columbus Avenue*

Modifiers of noun-headed structures of modification may consist of any of the modifiers that we have already found as modifiers of single-word heads in noun-headed structures of modification. And like the single-word heads, the noun-headed structure of modification may be the head of a number of modifiers:

For example, more than one single-word modifier:

Tribune	a syndicate bookie *counting house*
	Chicago's second *school budget*
Times	a short, silver-haired *Pentagon Admiral*
	the Bayaniban Philippine *dance company*
	the second annual *gymnastic entertainment*
Herald-Tribune	rococco old *Brooklyn Paramount*
Chronicle	gay, gaudy and glittering *international pageant*

Structures of coordination as modifiers of noun-headed structures of modification:

Times	sordid and dismembered *open space*

Modifiers may also consist of modifers which are themselves modified:

Times   Attorney (General) *Louis J. Lefkowitz*
                                 an average (of two) *bomb threats*
                                 assistant chief (of police) *John S. King*

Various combinations of single-word modifiers and structures of modification and coordination may also modify noun-headed structures of modification:

Times   Bing Crosby-Bob Hope *"Road" movies*
                     Central Young Men's *Christian Ass'n.*

Table 3 shows the distribution of the two types of heads: single-word noun-
heads and noun-headed structures of modification as heads. In 1894 single-
word heads represented about 83 to 84 per cent of the total and the noun-
headed structure of modification as head represented about 16 per cent of
the total. In 1964, however, there is an increase in the more complex structure
in which the head is itself a noun-headed structure of modification from
about 16 per cent of the total to about 22 per cent. Single-word modification
of single-word noun-heads, while somewhat lower than the 70 to 75 per cent
in 1894 is still roughly two-thirds of all modification where the head is a
noun or a noun sequence.

It is interesting to note also that while in representative sentences there
was a slight increase in the amount of modification of both types of heads,
in lead sentences there has been a slight drop in the amount of modification
of single-word heads and in the total number of single-word heads from
1894 to 1964.

I. CONCLUSIONS

Analysis of Tables 1, 2 and 3 will show some interesting things about noun-
headed structures of modification.

First of all, the distribution of the various modifiers as shown in Table 1
shows that nouns make up more than 50 per cent of all modifiers of noun-
heads, adjectives make up about 40 per cent, and adverbs and verbs together
represent only a little more than 2 per cent of all modifiers. Noun sequences,
that is noun-headed structures of modification, make up about 7 per cent
of the total of all modifiers of single-word noun-heads in 1964 in both representative sentences and lead sentences. In 1894 there were more than twice
as many sequences as modifiers in lead sentences as there were in representative sentences, but in 1964 there was practically no difference between
representative sentences and lead sentences.

Table 2 gives a breakdown of the various types of nouns that make up the
50 per cent of all modifiers of noun-heads in noun-headed structures of modi-

fication. In 1964 noun-adjuncts accounted for about two-thirds of the noun-modifiers, and function nouns as adjuncts accounted for roughly another 1 per cent. Possessives represent only 5 to 6 per cent of the total in 1964, a fact which suggests that the possessive suffix -'s is not a very useful means of identifying nouns.

Appositives represent about one quarter of all noun-modifiers in lead sentences and about one third of all noun-modifiers in representative sentences in 1964, totals which are slightly lower than those of 1894.

If we look at the breakdown of appositives by type, Table 2, we see an across-the-board drop in the use of titles from 1894 to 1964. This is probably, at least in part, accounted for by a less frequent use of *Mr.* with names today. Use of first names in both categories and in both years is fairly consistent, although there is something of a drop in representative sentences in 1964.

What is most interesting is the increase in the total number of noun-headed structures of modification from 1894 to 1964, shown in the totals in Table 1, and the increase in the total number of noun-adjuncts from 1894 to 1964, reflected in Table 2. The increase is seen, too, in both representative sentences and lead sentences. In representative sentences the increase in use of adjuncts was about 15 per cent and in lead sentences it is about 8 per cent. In number, however, adjuncts in representative sentences inceased by 211, and in lead sentences adjuncts increased by 161. Total increase in all nouns in modifying position in noun-headed structures of modification was 195 in representative sentences and 150 in lead sentences. Since the number of sentences in each category of the sample was the same in 1894 and in 1964, and the total number of words in each year was very much the same, the increase in noun-adjuncts from 1894 to 1964 seems significant.[28]

As Table 1 shows, other modifiers did not increase significantly, although there was a slight increase in adjective-modifiers in representative sentences in 1964, and although in percentages adjective-modifiers decreased slightly.

Table 3 shows the simplicity of the noun-headed structure of modification. The greatest number of modifiers of both single-word noun-heads and noun-headed structures of modification are single words. Sequences, primarily consisting of noun-headed structures of modification consisting of a single-word noun-head and a single-word modifier, represent a fairly small percentage of modifiers. A few coordinate sequences appear as modifiers, but other types of sequences are statistically infrequent.

[28] Total number of words for the two years were:

	representative	leads
1894	8,568	7,593
1964	8,485	7,021
minus	83	minus 572

III

NOUN-HEADED STRUCTURES OF MODIFICATION:
NOUN MARKERS

While noun markers, or determiners, are associated with nouns, Fries' Form Class 1 words, and with sequences and other words which replace nouns in characteristic noun positions, they are an optional feature, not an obligatory one. Their distribution is determined by lexical meaning, not by structure.

Table 4 shows the distribution of the various markers with noun-headed structures of modification, and Table 5 shows the distribution of noun markers with all other nouns, that is, with nouns not otherwise modified.

Noun markers fall into eight main groups: *the; a/an;* the various personal pronouns; the specifiers *this/that* and their plural forms *these/those;* cardinal numbers; the negative *no;* a fairly extensive list of what Francis terms function nouns; and the zero marker.

TABLE 4

Distribution of noun markers with noun-headed structures of modification in all newspapers in 1894 and 1964

Markers	Complete Stories				Leads Only			
	1894		1964		1894		1964	
	No.	%	No.	%	No.	%	No.	%
1. the	267	35.0	243	27.3	418	38.7	280	25.1
2. a/an	74	9.7	125	14.1	88	8.1	195	17.5
3. pronoun	24	3.1	32	3.6	22	2.0	36	3.2
4. specifier	3	.4	2	.2	4	.4	4	.4
5. numbers	11	1.4	46	5.2	23	2.1	66	5.9
6. negative	7	1.0	7	.7	3	.4	1	.1
7. other	10	1.3	4	.5	11	1.0	9	.8
total	396	51.9	459	51.6	569	52.7	591	53.0
8. zero	367	48.1	430	48.4	511	47.3	525	47.0
total	763	100.0	889	100.0	1080	100.0	1116	100.0

Francis divides the noun markers into only two groups, six words that serve only as noun markers and 19 that have other functions.[1] A more exhaustive examination is possible, however, if the markers are divided into the eight groups suggested here. All the noun markers except the articles *the* and *a/an* and the pronouns *my*, *your*, *our*, and *their* have other functions as well.[2] A more detailed description of the noun markers follows, with reference to Table 4.

Group 1 consists of the definite article *the:*

> *the* road
> *the* depression

Group 2 markers consists of the indefinite article *a* and its sandhi form *an:*

> *a* depot
> *an* office

Group 3 consists of pronouns. Four of these appear only as noun markers: *my*, *your*, *our*, *their*. Three others, *his*, *her*, *its*, appear also as function nouns:

> *his* work
> *its* solution
> *her* lecture
> *their* honeymoon
> *our* guests

Group 4 consist of the specifiers, *this* and *that*, and their plural forms, *these* and *those:*

> *this* meeting
> *that* day
> *these* securities

Group 5 consists of all cardinal numbers. These may be expressed as Arabic figures or as words, depending upon the arbitrary rules of usage, but any number from one up into the millions or billions is a determiner. Fractions are also considered markers:

> *50* dollars (usually written $50)
> *one* item
> *60,000* dollars
> *10,000,000* dollars

[1] *American English*, p. 237.
[2] *American English*, pp. 243—252; *Synopsis*, pp. 49—54.

nine schools

1/8 cent

Group 6 consists of the negative particle *no:*

no basis

no way

Group 7 consists of a number of function nouns. Francis, Nida, Strang, and Fries all list a number of these, and there are some differences in their lists.[3] For purposes of the present study, a check list was compiled of all the marker-function nouns listed by Francis, Nida, Strang, and Fries. Not all, of course, showed up in the materials under examination. Typical function nouns appearing as markers include:

many bosses

several conferences

each day

any proposal

much discussion

all nations

few people

Group 8 consists of only one marker, *zero*. Zero, of course, is not a marker, but the absence of a marker. To say that a noun has a zero marker is merely a handy way to state the structural fact that certain nouns never have a marker and other nouns, depending on lexical and structural circumstances, may not have a marker:[4] Names of people and certain geographical names do not have markers, for example, nor do some function nouns like *each* or *any* or *all*. In the materials examined in this study the following nouns of various types appeared without markers, that is, with a zero marker:

proper nouns

Illinois   Pennsylvania

Henry   Henneberry's

April

Faust

common nouns

steps   police

---

[3] *American English*, pp. 237—238 and 246—249; *Synopsis*, pp. 49—54; *Modern English*, pp. 109—115; *Structure*, pp. 88—89.

[4] Leonard Bloomfield gives a brief and clear picture of English noun classes based on whether they appear with markers or without. *Language* (New York, Holt, Rinehart and Winston, 1933, reprinted April 1962), p. 205.

    pupils   labor
    steamers   capital
    strikes   wheat
    saloons   death
    thought   property
    society   nature

function nouns

    these   few
    that   some
    one   each
    others

noun substitutes (pronouns)

    we   he
    it   themselves
    us

TABLE 5

Distribution of noun markers with otherwise unmodified nouns in all newspapers in 1894 and 1964

Markers	Complete Stories				Leads Only			
	1894		1964		1894		1964	
	No.	%	No.	%	No.	%	No.	%
the	421	33.7	257	22.5	419	34.3	211	22.1
a/an	77	6.2	107	9.3	110	9.1	95	9.9
pronoun	64	5.1	48	4.2	55	4.5	43	4.4
specifier	40	3.2	19	1.7	20	1.6	10	1.0
numbers	62	4.9	77	6.7	57	4.7	69	7.2
negative	12	.9	6	.5	3	.2	1	.1
other	34	2.7	21	1.8	36	2.9	17	1.7
total	710	56.7	535	46.9	700	57.3	446	46.7
zero	541	43.3	605	53.1	521	42.7	510	53.1
total	1251	100.0	1140	100.0	1221	100.0	956	100.0

Table, 5, which shows the distribution of markers with otherwise unmodified nouns, reveals that in 1964 in both representative and lead sentences more than 50 per cent of the unmodified nouns had a zero marker. These nouns, then, must be identified by some other signal than markers: position, possessive or plural inflection, derivational suffixes, or prosodic contrast. Table 6 presents a breakdown of these unmarked nouns and shows the number that are full nouns, function nouns, and noun substitutes, that is, pronouns.

TABLE 6

Distribution of nouns, pronouns, and function nouns appearing without noun markers in all newspapers in 1894 and 1964

	Complete Stories				Leads Only			
	1894		1964		1894		1964	
	No.	%	No.	%	No.	%	No.	%
Nouns	358	66.2	449	74.2	428	82.1	416	81.5
Pronouns	129	23.8	106	17.5	56	10.7	60	11.8
Function Nouns	54	9.9	50	8.3	37	7.1	34	6.7
total	541	99.9	605	100.0	521	99.9	510	100.0

Table 4 shows the same general distribution of markers with noun-headed structures of modification. Here slightly less than 50 per cent of the structures have a zero marker.

Tables 4 and 5 also show the relative frequency of the various markers. Zero outnumbers all other markers, the definite article *the* marks about one-quarter of all noun-headed structures of modification and unmodified nouns. All other markers appear relatively infrequently.

TABLE 7

Nouns not otherwise modified (including function nouns) and other form class words marked by noun markers in all newspapers in 1894 and 1964

	Complete Stories				Leads Only			
	1894		1964		1894		1964	
	No.	%	No.	%	No.	%	No.	%
Nouns	701	98.7	532	99.4	696	99.4	440	98.7
Other								
Adjectives	3	.4	2	.4	2	.3	6	1.3
Adverbs	2	.3	1	.2	—	—	—	—
Verbs	4	.6	—	—	2	.3	—	—
total	9	1.3	3	.6	4	.6	6	1.3
total	710	100.0	535	100.0	700	100.0	446	100.0

Table 7 shows the distribution of form class words other than nouns which appear in noun positions and are marked by nouns with markers other than zero. These are words like *best* and *latest* which are members of another form class, but substitute for a noun in certain circumstances. This is a relatively rare occurrence.

IV

NOUN-HEADED STRUCTURES OF MODIFICATION:
POST-NOMINAL MODIFIERS

Noun-headed structures of modification frequently consist of a noun-head, with or without pre-nominal modifiers, and with one or more modifiers appearing in a position after a noun-head. In the examples below, typical post-nominal modifiers, underlined, are shown with single-word noun heads. The whole is a structure of modification.

TABLE 8

Distribution of post-nominal modifiers in noun-headed structures of modification in all newspapers in 1894 and 1964

Modifiers	Complete Stories				Leads Only			
	1894		1964		1894		1964	
	No.	%	No.	%	No.	%	No.	%
Nouns								
appositives	38	5.4	78	10.3	56	5.7	94	10.4
numbers	16	2.3	25	3.3	16	1.6	32	3.5
other	21	3.0	45	6.0	40	4.1	51	5.6
total	75	10.7	148	19.6	112	11.4	177	19.5
Adjectives	18	2.6	8	1.1	12	1.2	19	2.9
Adverbs	7	1.0	5	.7	7	.7	10	1.1
Verbs								
present part	10	1.4	18	2.4	8	.8	14	1.5
past part	30	4.3	28	3.7	46	4.7	26	2.9
infinitive	12	1.7	19	2.5	12	1.2	19	2.1
total	52	7.4	65	8.6	66	6.7	59	6.5
Clauses	68	9.7	69	9.1	94	9.6	66	7.3
Prepositional Sequences	480	68.6	461	61.0	693	70.4	576	63.5
total	700	100.0	756	100.0	984	100.0	907	100.0

man *of the hour*
a boy *who likes candy*
a book *the same color*
the attorney *general*

In the post-nominal modifying position we find some of the modifiers already identified as pre-nominal modifiers: nouns, verbs, adjectives and adverbs. We also find some new structures and single words: prepositional sequences, noun sequences, verb + complement and object sequences, adjective + post-adjectival modifiers, and reflexive pronouns.

Table 8 shows the relative frequency and distribution of the various post-nominal modifiers in noun-headed structures of modification. Table 9 gives details as to the patterns of modification of noun-headed structures of modification with post-posed modifiers.

TABLE 9

Prior modification of noun-heads to which are added the various post-nominal modifiers shown in Table 8

Prior Modification	Complete Stories				Leads Only			
	1894		1964		1894		1964	
	No.	%	No.	%	No.	%	No.	%
No pre-modifiers	502	57.4	360	47.6	549	55.8	382	42.1
Pre-modifiers	215	30.7	272	36.0	322	32.8	385	42.4
Post-modifiers	63	9.0	63	8.3	65	6.6	64	7.1
Pre-modifiers and post-modifiers	20	2.9	61	8.1	48	4.9	76	8.4
total	700	100.0	756	100.0	984	100.1	907	100.1

A. ADJECTIVES AS POST-NOMINAL MODIFIERS

Adjectives appear as post-nominal modifiers in structures like the following:[1]

Nida   money *due*
              God *Almighty*
              time *immemorial*

Francis   court-*martial*
              grace *abounding*

[1] *Synopsis*, p. 88; *American English*, p. 298.

     fee *simple*
     darkness *visible*

Sometimes the modifying adjective has its own modifiers as in these examples where the modifiers are post-adjectival:[2]

  Nida   a person *desirous of a job*
         a man *anxious to get ahead*

In the four newspapers examined in this study, adjective-modifiers like the following were found:[3]

  Governer John B. Connally *Jr.*
  F. C. Carlucci *3rd*
  60 years *old*
  bid *sufficiently high*
  those *present*
  scores *more*
  diesases *incident to old age*
  consul *general*
  attorney *general*
  a city government *Republican in all its branches*
  profits *other than lawful interest*

B. ADVERBS AS POST-NOMINAL MODIFIERS

Adverbs occur as post-nominal modifiers, but not in any great numbers Table 8 shows. Nida and Francis cite these examples:[4]

  Nida   the space *below*
         the arc *above*
         this man *here*

  Francis   the heavens *above*
         Europe *now*
         the temperature *outside*

---

 [2] Synopsis, p. 89.
 [3] Examples from this point on will be merely representative of the whole sample of 300 sentences in each year and each category rather than representative of the individual newspapers. The fact that in so many instances the number of examples is relatively small and not distributed evenly across all four newspapers makes this a simpler means of citing examples.
 [4] *Synopsis*, p. 89; *American English*, p. 305.

In the four newspapers examined in this study, the following examples appeared:

> the campaign for social integration *here*
> with his fur *aflame*
> prices *generally*
> any day *now*
> the interview *yesterday*
> his defeat three years *ago*
> 2,430 *apiece*

C. VERBS AS POST-NOMINAL MODIFIERS

Verbs as post-nominal modifiers may take three forms: (1) the present participle; (2) the past participle; and (3) the marked infinitive. These post-posed verb-modifiers may appear alone or they may have their own modifiers.

Present participles as post-nominal modifiers, (a) alone, and (b) with their own modifiers:[5]

(a)	Nida	no man *living*
		the wisest man *breathing*
(b)	Nida	the person *trying to get this done*
		the boys *wishing to go*
	Francis	the water *running in the street*

Past participles as post-nominal modifiers, (a) appearing alone, and (b) with modifiers:[6]

(a)	Nida	the sum *required*
		the text *used*
		the results *obtained*
(b)	Nida	a man *accustomed to this*
	Francis	potatoes *baked slowly*

Marked infinitives as post-nominal modifiers, (a) appearing alone and (b) with a complement:[7]

(a)	Nida	the time *to go*
	Francis	money *to burn*
		the man *to see*
(b)	Nida	
	Francis	no examples

[5] *Synopsis*, p. 90; *American English*, p. 303.
[6] *Synopsis*, p. 90; *American English*, p. 303.
[7] *Synopsis*, p. 92; *American English*, p. 303.

In the four newspapers examined in this study verbs appeared as post-nominal modifiers in structures like the following:

present participles
    resolutions *expressing doubt*
    a map *showing the connections*
    evidence *regarding the cigarettes*
    procession *beginning at 9:25 a.m.*
    complaint *charging police brutality*

past participles
    trials *interrupted week before last*
    charges *made*
    a journal *devoted to all outdoor sports*
    a suit *brought by Estelle Pellit*
    meetings *being held*
    indictment *found against him*
    four men *exposed to severe radiation*

marked infinitives
    anything *to keep John Y. McKane out of Sing Sing prison*
    an heroic effort *to save itself*
    bills *to stimulate the construction*
    devices *to catch speeders*
    organization *to coordinate the campaign*

It will be noted that several of the verb-modifiers above have direct objects rather than modifiers: *to stimulate construction, to catch speeders*, for example.

D. CLAUSES AS POST-NOMINAL MODIFIERS

INCLUDED CLAUSES are structures that have the same form as statement sentences.[8] These sentences are preceded by a function word which we can call an INCLUDER, a word which serves to link the sentence to other structures or words. Included clauses consisting of an includer + sentence may be used to modify words and other structures including sentences and included clauses.

Included clauses used to modify nouns in noun-headed structures of modification are pretty much limited to those clauses whose includer is one of a small list of function words often called *relative pronouns*. Included clauses

---

[8] See *American English*, pp. 389—95, for a discussion of included clauses. Francis' definition of a statement sentence on which it is based depends on a number of structural patterns which he discusses on pages 379—80.

introduced by adverbial includers like *after, before, since, till, until, while* may occur as post-nominal modifiers, but they are not common.[9]

In the materials examined for this study, the most frequently appearing includers were *who* with its variants *whom* and *whose*, and *which* and *that*. Others appearing occasionally were *where, why,* and *when*.[10]

Examples of this kind of modification cited by Nida and Francis include:[11]

Nida the man *who failed to see it*[12]
the day *that I left*

Francis the fact *that it is raining*
the woman *whom he pointed out*

In the four newspapers examined in this study, included clauses appeared as modifiers in noun-headed structures of modification like the following:

Henry Mancini, *whose songs have won the Academy Award* . . .
suggestions *that the first trip to the moon may have to be delayed*
the likelihood *that there are other worlds*
golfers *who played at the Army-Navy club*
hundreds *whom the blizzard had kept indoors*
a man *whom he did not know*

In some instances, the includer is preceded by a preposition as in:[13]

Nida the man *to whom he gave the bill*
the story *to which he alluded*

PREPOSITIONS, not before defined in this study, are a class of function words preposed to nouns, primarily to link nouns to other words or structures. Fries, Francis, Nida, and Whitehall all contain lists of these function words.[14] In the present examples, the preposition appears preposed to a noun substitute — a relative pronoun — which is itself an includer linking a modifying structure to a head.

[9] *Synopsis*, pp. 99—100.
[10] For a more complete list of relative includers, see *Synopsis*, pp. 93—4, and *American English*, p. 393.
[11] *Synopsis*, pp. 94—97; *American English*, pp. 319 and 394.
[12] The relative includer frequently serves as both an includer and substitute for the noun-subject of the clause. See *American English*, pp. 393—4.
[13] *Synopsis*, p. 93; *American English*, p. 394.
[14] *Structure*, pp. 95—96; *American English*, pp. 305—311; *Synopsis*, pp. 205—6; and Whitehall, *Structural Essentials*, pp. 62—63.

Examples of preposition + includer as a link between clause and head from the four newspapers examined in this study:

> the case *in which a Park Avenue businessman has been accused of killing his bookmaker*
> art *for which this is the teaser*
> banquet *to which 25 sat down*
> Paige's hotel *into which he was taken from the street*
> the way *in which the modeling is suggested*
> hideaways *along which were stationed the servants*
> a description *of which appeared in the Tribune*

Quite often the clause is introduced by a zero includer:[15]

> Nida   the paper *I noticed*
>
> Francis   a place *he goes in summer*
>   the man *he told his story to*

In the newspapers examined for this study, the zero includer appears in structures like the following:

> the wound *he received when President Kennedy was assassinated*
> kindnesses *she had received*
> paper *you read*
> all *there is of the old Republican organization*

E. NOUNS AND NOUN SEQUENCES AS POST-NOMINAL MODIFIERS

Noun-headed structures of modification frequently consist of a noun-head or a noun-headed structure of modification modified by a single noun or a noun-headed structure of modification in post-nominal position. Like the nouns that appear in pre-nominal position, these post-nominal modifiers may be either a simple modifier or an appositive.

Francis and Nida give these examples of nouns or noun-headed structures of modification as post-nominal modifiers. In both instances, the sequences are appositives:[16]

> Nida   Jones, *the baker*
> Francis   Mr. Jones, *the art critic*

---

[15] *Synopsis*, p. 94; *American English*, pp. 398—9.
[16] *Synopsis*, p. 100; *American English*, p. 301.

Francis gives no examples of noun-headed structures of modification or nouns as post-nominal modifiers, not appositives, and Nida lists only those few which he calls quantitative or temporal modifiers:[17]

Nida   an animal *this size*
            a tree *that height*
            a woman *her age*
            the paper *this morning*

Single-word nouns marked by a determiner, like Nida's examples of appositives and modifiers, are not as common in post-nominal position as are noun-headed structures of modification. Examples of single-word modifiers, appositives and simple modifiers that do appear follow:

Vera Tischoff, *pianist*
another of his compositions, *"Charade"*
Glass, *a fireman*
Coleman and Wakefield, *agent*
Olshan and Gruendman, *attorneys*

We also find in post-nominal position what Nida calls semi-predicate attributives.[18] These are the reflexive pronouns like *myself, himself, herself* which appear in post-nominal position, but may also appear in other positions in the sentence:

Nida   I *myself* will try it
            I will *myself* try it
            I will try it *myself*

These reflexive pronouns are noun substitutes and here function as appositives. In the four newspapers examined, examples like the following occur:

the piece *itself*
work *itself*

Single-word nouns, simple modifiers not appositives, also appear in post-nominal position. Examples from the four newspapers examined include:

the Good Government Club *East*
Central Park *West*
the Eighth Ward, *Brooklyn*

[17] *Synopsis*, pp. 91—2.
[18] *Synopsis*, p. 103.

Salem, *Mass.*
Riverdale, *the Bronx*
Easton, *Pennsylvania*

Function nouns also appear as single-word post-nominal modifiers. The most common is a number. In the four newspapers examined in this study we find examples like:

Article *11.3*
Local *233*
March *14*
Smith, *35*

Much more common as post-nominal modifiers are noun-headed structures as modification. These may be either appositives or simple modifiers and may consist of noun-heads with pre-nominal modification, with post-nominal modification or with both. Examples from the four newspapers follow. Appositives:

Joseph F. Blaut, *ex-president of the Madison Square Bank*
counsel, *Gen. Benjamin F. Tracy*
wife, *the former Jeanne Jacchy*
Rolf Hochhuth, *author of "The Deputy"*
Evelyn Gamble Webster, *the wife of Burton C. Webster*
Thursday, *the day before a threatened mass resignation*
several amenities as a performer: *a strong left hand, a firm tone, a sweeping command of rhythm and, at times, a welcome sense of inner involvement*

Noun-headed structures of modification as simple modifiers, not appositives, include:

Governor John B. Connally of Texas, *his right arm in a cast from the wound he received when President Kennedy was assassinated*
the Parc Vendome, *340 West 57th Street*
two masked men, *one carrying a submachine gun*
the discontent of New York's night clubs *the past New Year weeks*
a scandal, *the first in its history*
a holdup . . .*yesterday afternoon*
George D. Hall, *65 years old*
the loss of the World Series *last October*
a witness *last fall*
Paige's hotel, *301 West Street*
photographs, *some in full color*

It should be noted that the post-nominal modifiers described above, single-word nouns and noun-headed structures of modification — some of which are appositives — are of two kinds: first, modifiers set off by commas from the head and the rest of the sentence, and, second, those without any intervening punctuation. The comma represents a distinct pause, a terminal juncture, in the spoken language which stands in distinct contrast to lack of such a pause in some structures.[19] Note the contrast in these examples:

the Parc Vendome, *340 West 57th Street*, where . . .
a witness *last fall* said that . . .

One rather peculiar structure of modification remains to be dealt with. This is a sequence consisting of *yesterday* or *tomorrow* as head with a post-posed noun modifier like *morning* or *afternoon*. For example:

yesterday *morning*
tomorrow *afternoon*
tomorrow *night*

These sequences are seldom further modified, although they may be; they never have a pre-posed marker; and they almost always appear in a sentence in an adverb position rather than in a noun position.

Tomorrow and *yesterday* without a post-posed modifier are clearly adverbs, but they may appear in noun-subject position as nouns and in this position be inflected like a noun. In this study we will follow Miss Strang in considering *tomorrow* and *yesterday* as noun-like words which have been derived from temporal adverbs.[20] This gets around the obvious difficulty that adverbs ordinarily are modified by nouns which are pre-posed, — not post-posed. If *yesterday* and *tomorrow* are nouns — at least in situations like this — then post-posed modifiers like *afternoon, morning*, and *night* are perfectly ordinary modifiers of nouns like the post-nominal modifiers just analyzed.

Having taken this position, the noun-headed structures of modification *yesterday + noun-modifier* and *tomorrow + noun-modifier* will be considered later as nouns when the various modifiers of verbs are analyzed.

Total number of these structures is not great. In 1894 there were 30 in lead sentences and eight in representative sentences. In 1964 there were 12 in lead sentences and five in representative sentences.

---

[19] For a discussion of juncture, see *American English*, pp. 155—57, and Trager and Smith, *Outline of English Structures*, pp. 41—52.
[20] *Modern English*, pp. 97—98.

F. PREPOSITIONAL SEQUENCES AS POST-NOMINAL MODIFIERS

The most common post-nominal modifier in noun-headed structures of modification is the sequence consisting of a preposition + a noun or a noun-
headed structure of modification. Nida and Francis cite these examples:[21]

Nida	*a piece of bread*
	a man in white
	the place across the water
Francis	*above suspicion*
	under water
	after dinner
	from the beginning
	like a thunderbolt

Prepositional sequences may consist of a preposition and a single-word
noun or noun-headed structure of modification. Or the place of the noun
may be taken, upon occasion, by a verb, an adjective, an adverb, a function
noun or pronoun, or by a prepositional sequence.[22]

Examples of prepositional sequences as post-nominal modifiers in the four
newspapers examined in this study include:

one *of the six presidents*
section *of the city*
witness *in his murder trial*
trial *upon an indictment*
dogs *in Madison Square Garden*
ten years *at hard labor*
building *at Twenty-Third Street*
floor *of the assembly*

Post-nominal modification has some interesting aspects. First of all, it
shows a radical departure from pre-nominal modification where the principal
modifier, referring back to Tables 1 and 2, were single words. In post-nominal
modification, as Tables 8 and 9 show, more than two-thirds of the modifiers
are prepositional sequences, structures of several words and varying complexity
rather than a single word. As we shall see later in analyses of other structures
of modification, the prepositional sequence is the most used of all modifiers
in present-day English. Secondly, it is interesting to note what a small part
all other modifiers play. Nouns amount to roughly 20 per cent of the post-

---

[21] *Synopsis*, pp. 90—91; *American English*, p. 309.
[22] *American English*, pp. 305—11; *Synopsis*, pp. 205—7.

nominal modifiers in 1964, a substantial increase over their use in 1894. All other modifiers, verbs, adjectives, adverbs, and clauses, represent less than 20 per cent of modifiers post-posed to noun-heads.

The increase in nouns as post-posed modifier of noun-heads in 1964 newspapers is countered by a roughly similar decrease in the number of prepositional sequences in use in 1964 newspapers.

Table 9 shows that somewhat better than one third of all noun-heads which have a single post-posed modifiers also have pre-posed modifiers. About the same number have no pre-posed modifiers except markers and only a single post-posed modifier. Some 7 or 8 per cent of the noun-heads have more than one post-posed modifier, but no pre-posed modifiers, and about 8 per cent have pre-posed modifiers and more than one post-posed modifier.

V

VERB-HEADED STRUCTURES OF MODIFICATION

In a structure of modification in which the verb is head, the various modifiers may appear in three positions adjacent to the verb-head: pre-posed, post-posed, or within the verb sequence between the auxiliary and the main verb. Verb-modifiers also appear, but less frequently than they appear in the positions just mentioned, in a position separated from the verb-head by the object or complement of the verb-head.

Table 10 shows the distribution of modifiers in these positions in the materials examined for this study. As the table shows, more than twice as many modifiers appear adjacent to the verb-head as appear separated by an object or complement. This is true in all the newspapers examined and for both years, and also holds true for both representative sentences and lead sentences. The proportion of modifiers that appear pre-posed to the verb or within the verb sequence is smallest of all, as Table 10 shows.

TABLE 10

Position of modifiers of verbs, including verb and complement or object, in all newspapers in 1894 and 1964

| Position | Complete Stories | | | | Leads Only | | | |
| | 1894 | | 1964 | | 1894 | | 1964 | |
	No.	%	No.	%	No.	%	No.	%
Pre-verb	30	4.7	40	6.0	47	5.8	41	4.6
Within the Verb Sequence	49	7.6	23	3.4	44	5.4	23	2.6
Post-verb	388	60.2	409	60.4	484	59.6	527	59.5
total	467	72.4	472	69.7	575	70.8	591	66.7
Post Complement or Object	178	27.6	205	30.3	237	29.2	295	33.3
total	645	100.0	677	100.0	812	100.0	836	100.0

A. MODIFIERS ADJACENT TO THE VERB-HEAD

Modifiers appearing pre-posed to the verb-head, as cited by Francis and Nida:[1]

    Francis   *successfully* tried
                      slowly drove

    Nida   *continually* wanted
                     accidentally shot

Modifiers appearing within the verb sequence between the auxiliary and the main verb, as cited by Francis and Nida:[2]

    Francis   has *sometimes* seen
                      has *seldom* been heard

    Nida   were *actually* compelling
                      had *never* ridden

Modifiers appearing post-posed to a verb-head, as cited by Francis and Nida:[3]

    Francis   works *successfully*
                      stepped *inside*

    Nida   sat *reading*
                      stared *fascinated*

These last, modifiers post-posed to the verb-head, appear actually in three different environments: (1) after a transitive verb and before the direct object or indirect object or both; (2) sentence-final after an intransitive verb; and (3) after a linking verb and before the complement. Examples of post-posed modifiers of transitive verb-heads where the modifier appears between the verb-head and the verb's object:[4]

    He felt *keenly* his inability
    He studied *attentively* the program of procedure.

The post-posed, sentence-final modifier of an intransitive verb-head:[5]

    They came back *wounded*.
    He went off *a happy man*.

[1] *American English*, p. 315: *Synopsis*, p. 138.
[2] *American English*, p. 315; *Synopsis*, p. 138.
[3] *American English*, p. 314; *Synopsis*, p. 157.
[4] *Synopsis*, p. 139.
[5] *Synopsis*, pp. 157—58.

The post-posed modifier of a linking verb-head appearing between the linking verb and its complement:[6]

He is *naturally* a very timid person.
She is *sometimes* quite charming.

B. AFTER THE COMPLEMENT OR OBJECT

Quite frequently, as Table 10 shows, modifiers of the verb appear after the complement of a linking verb or after the object of a transitive verb; in the following example, cited by Francis, after a linking verb and its complement:[7]

It is dark *ahead*.

After the object of a transitive verb; as cited by Nida:[8]

They saw them *frequently*.
They planned it *carefully yesterday*.

There may be some ambiguity when modifiers appear after a complement or object, but it probably can be assumed that the modifier is following a head consisting of a verb and complement or object. In the sentence *It is dark ahead*, Francis says that the adverb *ahead* modifies the linking verb and its subjective complement together.[9] And although he does not specifically say so, Francis' diagrams of transitive sentences indicate that he considers modifiers in this position to modify both head and object.[10] Nida calls all modifiers of verb-heads, no matter what their position, '3rd type attributives (modifiers) of the verb-head'.[11] He nowhere mentions the problem of the intervening object or complement in sentences like those just cited. In this study it is assumed that the modifiers appearing after a verb and its object or complement are somewhat different from modifiers appearing in positions adjacent to the verb-head. These two types of heads, verb-head and verb + complement or object-head, are tabulated separately (See Tables 11 and 13), but essentially they differ only in position of the modifier and in the fact that in one instance the modifier modifies the verb and perhaps some other modifiers, and in the other it modifies the verb and a complement or object.

[6] *Synopsis*, p. 139.
[7] *American English*, p. 321.
[8] *Synopsis*, pp. 139—40.
[9] *American English*, p. 321.
[10] *American English*, p. 314.
[11] *Synopsis*, p. 136.

C. MODIFIERS OF VERB-HEADS

Modifiers of verb-heads when they appear in positions adjacent to the verb-head include adjectives, adverbs, verbs, clauses, prepositional sequences, and nouns and noun sequences. Examples of nouns as modifiers of verb-heads, as cited by Francis and Nida, include:[12]

Francis	lived *a year*
	saw *a mile*
Nida	*this year* exceeded our limit
	died *a beggar*

Examples of adjectives as modifiers of verb-heads as cited by Francis and Nida include:[13]

Francis	ran *true*
	went *crazy*
	fell *flat*
Nida	talks *big*
	stop *dead*
	sweep *clean*

Examples of adverbs as modifiers of verb-heads as cited by Francis and Nida include:[14]

Francis	drives *rapidly*
	stepped *inside*
Nida	*continually* wanted
	were *actually* compelling

Examples of verbs as modifiers of verb-heads as cited by Francis and Nida include:[15]

Francis	came *running*
	eat *sitting*
	lives *to eat*
	came *to scoff*

[12] *American English*, p. 317; *Synopsis*, p. 143.
[13] *American English*, p. 318; *Synopsis*, p. 156.
[14] *American English*, p. 134; *Synopsis*, p. 137.
[15] *American English*, p. 318; *Synopsis*, pp. 156—59.

Nida   went *equipped*
          stared *fascinated*
          came back *wounded*

          came *running*
          went on *working*
          lay *gasping*

          ache *to think of it*
          aspire *to see him*
          get *to go*
          grow *to be a man*

Examples of clauses as modifiers of verb-heads, as cited by Francis:[16]

Francis   came *after I left*
          will go *wherever you go*

Nida says that clauses may modify verb-heads in any of the positions already mentioned, but his examples represent only what in this study is taken to be a different kind of modification: modification of sentence-heads. This type of modification will be discussed in the next chapter.[17]

Prepositional sequences as modifiers of verb-heads, as cited by Francis and Nida:[18]

Francis   spoke *about his work*
          entered *into the game with gusto after dinner*

Nida   will *by all means* undertake the work
          is *in general* quite pleased

D. MODIFIERS OF VERB AND OBJECT

All the modifiers just cited, nouns and noun sequences, adjectives, verbs, clauses and prepositional sequences, may appear in final position in the sentence where they are separated from the verb-head by the verb's object or complement. For example:

killed two employes *last year*
will address a special meeting *tomorrow night*

---

[16] *American English*, p. 318.
[17] *Synopsis*, p. 145.
[18] *American English*, p. 319; *Synopsis*, p. 136.

Since the modifiers appearing in this position are the same modifiers already described, there is no need to cite further examples as models.

Table 11 shows the distribution of these various modifiers of verb-heads in all newspapers in both 1894 and 1964 in both lead sentences and representative sentences. The table shows a modest increase in the total number of modifiers in representative sentences from 1894 to 1964 and a slightly larger, though still modest, increase in the modification of verb-heads in lead sentences over the same period.

There are so few modifiers of each type that it is difficult to draw conclusions. The relatively large number of adverbs is to be expected, but again the prepositional sequence ranks ahead of all other modifiers. The increase in the number of adverbs and noun sequences in lead sentences in 1964 can be accounted for by an increased use of adverbs like *today* and *yesterday* and noun sequences like *last night* in lead sentences.

TABLE 11

The various modifiers of verb-heads in all newspapers in 1894 and 1964

| | Complete Stories | | | | Leads Only | | | |
| | 1894 | | 1964 | | 1894 | | 1964 | |
	No.	%	No.	%	No.	%	No.	%
Nouns and Noun Sequences	24	5.2	26	5.5	59	10.3	45	7.6
Adjectives	12	2.5	7	1.5	9	1.5	—	—
Adverbs	135	28.9	146	51.3	148	25.7	230	38.7
Verbs								
present part	4	.8	2	.4	3	.5	5	.8
past part	—	—	2	.4	—	—	2	.3
infinitive	8	1.7	14	2.9	8	1.3	15	2.5
total	12	2.5	18	3.8	11	1.9	22	3.7
Clauses	20	4.2	17	3.6	15	2.6	19	3.2
Prepositional Sequences	264	56.5	258	54.7	333	57.9	267	45.2
total	467	99.8	472	99.9	575	99.9	591	98.6

E. EXAMPLES FROM THE NEWSPAPERS

In the materials examined in this study most modifiers of verb-heads appeared post-posed, as Table 10 shows. Examples of modifiers in this position will be given first, followed by examples of modifiers pre-posed and within the sequence. Examples of modifiers appearing post-posed to the verb and its object or complement will follow.

Modifiers of verb-heads post-posed:

(nouns and noun sequences)

> flew *this week*
> sold *last week*
> will travel *each day*
> lasted *50 minutes*
> was killed *last Tuesday*
> filed *yesterday morning*

(adjectives)

> pleaded *guilty*
> keeping *silent*
> has kept *hush-hush*

(adverbs)

> was arrested *yesterday*
> has been seen *here*
> warned *here*
> will be put into operation *today*
> played *a few days ago*

(verbs)

> car radioed *to have the motorist arrested*
> sat up Sunday night *to attend his sick wife*
> gathered *to celebrate the 25th anniversary*
> went there *to collect $25,000*
> were going around the ward yesterday *begging votes* . . .
> will be presented *beginning March 4*
> is confined *suffering from a fractured ankle*
> was found *stabbed to death*
> was found *raped and beaten*

(clauses)

> received *when President Kennedy was assassinated*
> flew into New York *as another of his compositions was named* . . .
> was performed *while she was under the influence of a drug*
> has been living quietly *since she came from France*
> is obtained *when she stands up*

(prepositional sequences)

> can be found *in New York*
> were announced *by the Health Department*
> has been pulsing *with steady business*
> died at *Lenox Hill Hospital*

responded *like an old firehorse*
will be celebrated *until today's sunset*

In the newspapers examined in this study, modifiers of the verb-head appeared pre-posed in instances like the following:

(nouns and noun sequences)

> *last night* said
> *last Saturday* night was critically injured
> *last year* decided
> *yesterday morning* heard

(adjectives)

> *first* gave

(adverbs)

> *yesterday* criticized
> *still* lack
> *any day now* may reach
> *firmly* grounded
> *then* spent

(verbs)

> no examples

(clauses)

> *exactly as he foretold* drew

(prepositional sequences)

> *by so doing* attracted
> *with permission of relatives* removed
> *in the Court of Common Pleas* handed down
> *of a somewhat different nature* have been
> *through his counsel* pleaded
> *behind batteries of champagne on St. Patrick's Day* boast
> *on a southern reef* is moldering

Examples of modifiers appearing within the verb sequence are less frequent, but the following were found in the materials examined in this study:

(adverbs)

> can be *unreservedly* congratulated
> have *long* remembered
> is *not* coming
> would *soon* become

appeared *yesterday* to be setting

may *also* send

(prepositional sequences)

was *according to the records of the box office* visited

was *at once* arrested

has *at last* settled down

would *in no way* advance

was *at first* supposed

As some of the examples cited above indicate, more than one modifier frequently modifies a single verb-head. For example, a verb-head with a post-posed modifier may also have a pre-posed modifier or a modifier within the verb sequence:

are *not* entitled *to the aid*

is *not* coming *to the United States*

was *well* received *at a public hearing*

can *not* say *definitely*

firmly grounded *in no-nonsense mud*

ever seen *West of Chicago*

not to go *outside the theater*

last Saturday evening was *critically* injured

Where the verb-head is modified only by post-posed modifiers, it is common to have two or more such modifiers. To have three post-posed modifiers modifying a single verb-head is not uncommon; more can be found occasionally, but multiple modification is generally limited to two modifiers or three modifiers:

ran *back and forth between the terminals in large, shrieking groups*

howled *dismally through the ruins yesterday*

was found *by police hanging from a flagpole in the Civic Center near Grove and Park streets about 3:15 a.m. yesterday*

met *yesterday with Clair M. Reddiwig to discuss the civil rights boycott in a secret session*

worked *14 years for the Lerner newspapers also*

was found *dead in bed in his room at No. 825 Milwaukee Avenue last evening*

responded *like an old firehorse yesterday to the sound of an alarm*

Table 12 shows the distribution of multiple modifiers in the materials examined. Multiple modification, as the table shows, is much less frequent than modification of a verb-head by a single modifier.

TABLE 12

Incidence of single and multiple modification of verb-heads in all newspapers in 1894 and in 1964

	Complete Stories				Leads Only			
	1894		1964		1894		1964	
	No.	%	No.	%	No.	%	No.	%
One Modifier	156	58.6	150	56.0	183	54.1	187	53.0
Two Modifiers	75	28.3	75	28.0	93	27.5	137	38.8
Three Modifers	28	10.6	34	12.7	46	13.7	48	13.6
Four Modifiers	4	1.5	7	2.6	10	2.9	9	2.5
More Than Four Modifiers	2	.8	2	.7	4	1.1	2	.6

Table 13 shows that even where there is more than one modifier the range is extremely limited. In by far the greatest number of instances of multiple modification, the verb-head has only two modifiers. Three modifiers are less frequent and in only a few instances do we find four or more modifiers of a verb-head.

TABLE 13

Incidence of single and multiple modification of verb-heads in all newspapers in 1894 and in 1964

	Complete Stories		Leads Only	
	1894	1964	1894	1964
Total Heads	265	268	338	353
Total Modifiers	467	472	575	527
Single Modifiers	156	150	183	187
Multiple Modifiers	109	118	155	166

F. VERB AND OBJECT AS HEAD

Somewhere between a quarter and a third of all modifiers of verb-heads appear in a position apart from the head and separated from it by the verb-head's object or objects or its complement. Examples of the various modifiers appearing in this position in the materials examined in this study follow:

(nouns and noun sequences)

will address the monthly meeting *Wednesday*

took place *this morning*
took over classrooms *last week*
killed two employes *last year*
will address a special meeting *tomorrow night*
took part *February 3*
cut revenue *$13 million*

(adjectives)

no examples

(adverbs)

resumed an inquiry *yesterday*
picked up the telephone *yesterday*
slugging it *out*
gave some things *away*
afflicting the South *now*
made a surprise raid *two weeks ago*
has been a good demand *recently*

(verbs)

induces children *to stay out of school*
were offered $20,000 *to turn their backs*
has been raising funds *to restore the old theater*
asked police *to get back his $200*

to have the marriage *annulled*
was fourth *lapped on Lucinda*
was a prisoner *charged with disorderly conduct*

found himself *fighting a blaze of scandal*

(clauses)

to stage a work stoppage *should a Senate fillibuster break out*
was declared a deserter *after he left Fort Bragg*
would assist the strike *if it were called*
to tell anything *when she saw fit*
kept the adrenalin gushing *until she was recalled*
stabbed a woman friend to death *because he was executing the will of
God*
was an awful tomboy *when I was a little girl*
was dead *before the doctor could be of any help*

(prepositional sequences)

taking sides *in a preliminary contest*
driving a stolen car *across the state*
to keep themselves *in power*

was fresh snow *on the ground*

returned the ordinance *without his approval*

asking $200,000 *for alleged alienation*

Table 14 shows the distribution of the various modifiers of verb-heads when they appear apart from the head and following the verb-head's object or complement. During the 70-year period from 1894 to 1964 there was a significant increase in the total number of modifiers of verb-heads in this position in both lead sentences and representative sentences, an increase that was somewhat greater than was found among modifiers appearing in positions adjacent to the verb-head.

TABLE 14

The various modifiers of verb + object or complement-heads in all newspapers in 1894 and in 1964

	Complete Stories				Leads Only			
	1894		1964		1894		1964	
	No.	%	No.	%	No.	%	No.	%
Nouns and Noun								
Sequences	6	3.4	9	4.4	33	13.9	30	10.2
Adverbs	29	16.3	23	11.2	33	13.9	62	21.0
Verbs								
present part	—	—	—	—	1	.4	2	.6
past part	2	1.1	—	—	1	.4	—	—
infinitive	8	4.5	14	6.8	5	2.1	17	5.8
total	10	5.6	14	6.8	7	3.0	19	6.4
Clauses	16	9.0	15	7.3	15	6.3	19	6.4
Prepositional								
Sequences	117	65.7	144	70.2	149	62.9	165	56.0
total	178	100.0	205	99.7	237	100.0	295	100.0

Among representative sentences, most of the modifiers showed some increase, but there was a slight drop in the number of adverbs appearing as modifiers. Among lead sentences, the modifiers which gained the most were adverbs, nearly doubled in use, and infinitives. Prepositional sequences in both lead sentences and representative sentences gained slightly. All these increases were too large to be accounted for by chance.

It is interesting to note that here again the most common modifier is the prepositional sequence that in both lead sentences and representative sentences in both years equals or exceeds in number all other modifiers combined. This is particularly interesting in the light of statements by Francis that the position here dominated by the prepositional sequence is the typical adverb position.[19] Francis calls this utterance-final position after a noun or nouns the principal adverb position. Ability to fill this position is the primary structural criterion for adverbs, Francis says.[20] As a matter of fact, as a comparison of Tables 11 and 14 will show, prepositional sequences outnumber adverbs as modifiers of verb-heads in every position, and there are from four to five times as many adverbs post-posed to verb-heads as appear in Francis' typical adverb position after the verb-head and its object or complement.

At least in the materials examined in this study, it would appear that the structurally most significant adverb position is the position immediately after the verb-head. More adverbs are found in this position than in any other.

TABLE 15

Incidence of single and multiple modification of verb + object-complement heads in all newspapers in 1894 and in 1964

	Complete Stories		Leads Only	
	1894	1964	1894	1964
Total Heads	128	172	155	183
Total Modifiers	178	205	237	295
Single Modifiers	86	126	95	98
Multiple Modifiers	42	46	60	85

It is quite common to find more than one modifier of the verb-head and its object or complement occupying this utterance- (sentence-) final position as Tables 15 and 16 show. Table 15 shows that single modifiers are more common than multiple modification in representative sentences, but that in lead sentences there is a trend toward multiple modification. As Table 16 shows, two modifiers are most common. More than two are infrequent.

Examples of multiple modification of the type summarized in Tables 15 and 16 include:

> helped Jews and other refugees *in a skylight apartment in Rome during the German occupation*
> stabbed his teacher *in the back with a penknife yesterday morning before the start of classes.*
> opened his second season *last night at the new hall in 40th Street near Broadway*

[19] *American English*, p. 281.
[20] *American English*, p. 281.

There is some question in these instances of multiple modification whether the succeeding modifiers are independent modifiers of the head, or whether they modify the head and the intervening modifiers. Probably both situations exist, and although there is some structural ambiguity here, meaning is usually quite clear.

TABLE 16

Incidence of single and multiple modification of verb + complement or object heads in all newspapers in 1894 and in 1964

	Complete Stories				Leads Only			
	1894		1964		1894		1964	
	No.	%	No.	%	No.	%	No.	%
One Modifier	86	67.2	126	73.3	95	61.3	98	53.6
Two Modifiers	34	26.6	40	23.3	44	28.4	62	33.9
Three Modifiers	8	6.2	5	2.9	12	7.7	20	10.9
Four Modifiers	—	—	1	.6	3	1.9	2	1.1
Five Modifiers	—	—	—	—	—	—	1	.5
More Than Five Modifiers	—	—	—	—	1	.6	—	—

VI

OTHER STRUCTURES OF MODIFICATION

A. ADJECTIVE-HEADED STRUCTURES

Adjectives, like nouns and verbs, may be head of a structure of modification. However, as Table 17 shows, such adjective-headed structures of modification are few in number, and the range of modifiers is more restricted than is the case where the head of a structure of modification is a noun or a verb.

The principal modifiers of adjectives are adverbs and prepositional sequences. Adjectives may also be modified by verbs, by clauses, and occasionally by nouns. In the materials examined for this study, no other modifiers appeared.

Modifiers of adjectives appeared pre-posed and post-posed to their head, as the examples which follow will show. Pre-posed modifiers may include adverbs, nouns, verbs and other adjectives, according to examples cited by Nida and Francis. Examples of adverbs as modifiers of adjective-heads:[1]

TABLE 17

Modification of adjectives in all newspapers in 1894 and in 1964

Modifiers	Complete Stories				Leads Only			
	1894		1964		1894		1964	
	No.	%	No.	%	No.	%	No.	%
Adverbs	18	43.9	16	45.7	22	42.3	19	43.2
Verbs	3	7.3	2	5.7	6	11.5	3	6.8
Clauses	3	7.3	1	2.8	4	7.7	—	—
Prepositional Sequences	17	41.5	15	42.8	19	37.5	21	47.7
total	41	100.0	35*	99.8	52*	100.0	44*	100.0

* Includes one function noun.

[1] *Synopsis*, p. 163; *American English*, pp. 320—321.

Francis   (the) _____ famous singer
                    exceedingly
                    somewhat
                    always
                    still

Nida   *about* sick
               absurdly fanciful
               quite right
               less appealing

In the materials examined in this study, the following examples appeared

    personally liable
    much excited
    too severe
    sharply higher
    better known
    not guilty
    utterly dead
    increasingly still
    very dormant

Several of the modifiers noted here, *very, too, much,* and there are others, are on Fries' list of Group D function words, function words he calls *degree words* and which Francis refers to as *qualifiers.*[2] Structurally, these degree words do not differ from other adverbs, (in some instances from nouns) and there are so few of them in the materials examined in this study that it was decided not to consider them apart from other adverbs. They will appear again as modifiers of adverb-heads and the same situation exists there.

Nouns appearing alone or marked by determiners, and noun sequences also appear as modifiers in adjective-headed structures of modification. Nida and Francis cite the following examples:[3]

Francis   *stone* cold
               sea green
               bone dry

Nida   *that* young
               that sick
               a few months old
               nany times finer

[2] *Structure*, pp. 92—94.
[3] *Synopsis*, p. 164; *American English*, p. 321.

Only three examples of this type of modification appear in the materials examined in this study:

> *a bit* difficult
> *100 per cent* better
> *8 centuries* old

Verbs also appear as modifiers in adjective-headed structures of modification, but again, this is not a common pattern. Nida and Francis cite the following examples:[4]

Francis	*freezing* cold
	boiling hot
	hopping mad
Nida	*passing* fair
	chilling cold

Not a single instance of a verb as pre-posed modifier of an adjective-head was found in the materials examined in this study.

Francis also cites examples of adjectives as modifiers in adjective-headed structures of modification, structures like *icy cold*, but none were found in this study.[5]

Modifiers in post-adjective position were more common in the materials examined in this study; these post-posed modifiers included verbs, prepositional sequences and clauses. Examples of verbs as post-posed modifiers of adjective-heads, as cited by Nida and Francis, are:[6]

Francis	hard *to get*
	beautiful *to see*
	easy *to know*
Nida	able *to do it*
	accustomed *to see*
	ambitious *to get it done*

Examples of this type of modification appearing in the materials examined in this study include:

> able *to order*
> convenient *to let him*

---

[4] *Synopsis*, p. 165; *American English*, p. 321.
[5] *American English*, p. 322.
[6] *American English*, p. 322; *Synopsis*, p. 165.

curious *to see*
sufficient *to cause another cent break*
unwilling *to render the slightest assistance*

Neither Francis nor Nida cited an example of an adjective-head with a post-posed participial modifier, but one example appeared in the materials examined in this study:

worth *relating*

The adverb *enough* may appear as a post-posed modifier of an adjective, as in *true enough*, but no example was found in the materials examined in this study.[7]

The prepositional sequence appears almost as frequently as the adverb as a modifier of adjective-heads. In the materials examined in this study, 76 adverbs appeared as modifiers of adjective-heads and 72 prepositional sequences appeared as modifiers of adjective-heads. The adverbs were all pre-posed modifiers and the prepositional sequences were all post-posed modifiers. Examples of prepositional sequences as adjective-modifiers, as cited by Francis and Nida:[8]

Francis   easy *on the eyes*
               good *for nothing*
               stronger *than ever*

Nida   glad *of it*
               short *in stature*
               inferior *to him*
               dependent *upon him*

In the materials examined in this study, the following examples of prepositional sequences as modifiers of adjective-heads appear:

devoted *to the interests*
liable *for any debt*
consistent *with the interests*
larger *than that*
incident *to old age*
last *of the "Flying Farnums"*
overburdened *with lands*
city-wide *in membership*

[7] *Synopsis*, p. 163.
[8] *American English*, p. 322; *Synopsis*, p. 167.

Occasionally an adjective-head is separated from its modifier, as in these examples cited by Nida.[9] The adjective-head is in small capitals and the modifying prepositional sequence is in italics:

> very SIMILAR propositions *to these*
> a very DIFFERENT matter *from applause*

One example of this variant type of adjective-headed structure of modification appeared in the materials examined in this study:

> a RARE accolade *for an author*

The clauses that appear as modifiers in adjective-headed structures of modification are of several types. First is the clause marked by the includers *what, that, if, when, where, who, how, why, which, whether* and by zero. Nida cites the following examples:[10]

> I am afraid *he is here.*
> He was so boastful *that he could do it.*
> Some were uncertain *whether they should go.*

In the materials examined in this study, the following examples of clauses as post-posed modifiers of adjective-heads were found:

> to make sure (that) *they do not support firms that discriminate*
> became so much excited *that he took measures* . . .
> The security . . . is so tight *that for nearly three years it has kept hush-hush a crime* . . .

The adjective-head in structures of modification like these is frequently conditioned or marked by a preposed adverb, *so:*[11]

> *so* dense *that the diners were forced to leave the room*
> *so* meager *that almost no business was possible*
> *so* tight *that for nearly three years it was kept hush-hush*

Than or *as* also serve as markers for clauses modifying adjective-heads. Nida cites the following examples:[12]

> better *than we thought*
> such *as these men described*

---

[9] *Synopsis,* p. 91.
[10] *Synopsis,* p. 166.
[11] *Synopsis,* p. 166—67.
[12] *Synopsis,* pp. 166—67.

In the materials examined in this study, the following examples of this type of adjective-headed structure of modification were found:

> such *as we desired*
> greater *than characterized the plays*

In some instances when the modifying clause is introduced by *than* or *as*, the adjective-head has a pre-posed conditioner or marker. When the modifying clause is introduced by *as*, the conditioner or marker is either *as* or *so:*

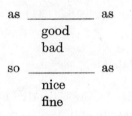

When the modifying clause is introduced by *than*, the conditioner or marker is *more* or *less* or an adverb inflected with the comparative suffix *-er:*

> more _____ than
> _____ -er _____ than

Nida cites the following examples of this type of modification of adjective heads:[13]

> *more* thoughtful *than the others*
> *as* quiet *as Dick*

Examples of this type of adjective-headed structure of modification found in the materials examined in this study include:

> *as* controversial *as the first*
> *as* significant *as it was unique*

As Table 18 shows, slightly more than half the modifiers of adjective-heads are post-posed. The largest group of modifiers, adverbs, are pre-posed, except for the adverb *enough*. The second largest group of modifiers, the prepositional sequence, always is post-posed.

---

[13] *Synopsis*, pp. 166—67.

TABLE 18

Distribution of modifiers of adjectives in all newspapers in 1894 and in 1964

Position	Complete Stories				Leads Only			
	1894		1964		1894		1964	
	No.	%	No.	%	No.	%	No.	%
Pre-adjective	16	38.1	15	42.9	22	43.1	17	38.6
Post-adjective	26	61.9	20	57.1	29	56.9	27	61.4
total	42	100.0	35	100.0	51	100.0	44	100.0

B. ADVERB-HEADED STRUCTURES

Adverb-headed structures of modification are similar to the adjective-headed structures of modification. Modifiers appear pre-posed and post-posed and include nouns and noun sequences, adverbs, clauses, verbs and prepositional sequences. Adjectives do not appear as modifiers of adverb-heads.

The pre-posed modifiers are adverbs, nouns and noun sequences like the following examples cited by Nida and Francis.[14] First, adverbs as modifiers:

Francis	*unusually* eagerly
	far away
	sometimes below
	rather slowly
Nida	*extremely* hard

In the materials examined in this study, the following examples of adverb as modifiers of adverb-heads were found:

early yesterday
still on
as quickly
shortly thereafter
not easily
again yesterday
once again
just exactly
certainly not

[14] *Synopsis*, pp. 141—43; *American English*, p 323.

Some of these adverb-modifiers appear on Fries' list of Group D degree words: *just*, *still*, for example — but so few of the Group D words appear as modifiers that they are lumped here with other adverb-modifiers.

Nouns and noun sequences frequently appear as modifiers of adverb-heads:[15]

Francis   *a foot* away
                that easily
                some way up

Nida   *a lot* better
                a great deal sooner
                ten feet further

Examples of this type of modification appearing in the materials examined in this study include:

a year ago
a shade lower
a short time ago
seconds later
all day yesterday
a couple of blocks away
share and share alike
a year later

Post-posed modifiers of adverb-heads include prepositional sequences and clauses. Nida cites examples of verbs as post-posed modifiers of adverb-heads, structures like *sufficiently to be noticed*, but none were found in the materials examined in this study.[16] Examples of prepositional sequences as post-posed modifiers of adverb-heads, as cited by Francis and Nida include:[17]

Francis   away *for a week*
                behind *in his work*
                outside *in the cold*

Nida   luckily *for him*
                far *from here*
                near *to the place*

Examples of this type of modification as found in the materials examined in this study include:

[15] *American English*, p. 323; *Synopsis*, p. 141.
[16] *Synopsis*, p. 143.
[17] *Synopsis*, p. 143; *American English*, p. 323.

out *of classes*
unfortunately *for him*
ahead *of Sacramento*
back *to their kennels and home*
here *within reach*
out *of the city*
later *on in the day*

Clauses also may appear as modifiers of adverb-heads, as the following examples from Nida indicate:[18]

here *where the church stood*
once *when the preacher coughed*
so frequently *that he completely destroyed the power of resistance*
as fast *as he could*
more frequently *than the rest*

Clauses modifying adverb-heads pattern like the clauses that modify adjective-heads.[19] Examples of this type of modification as found in the materials examined in this study include:

so much *as they were*
as effectively *as it sells a product*
as rapidly *as some climb*
so slow *that some clubs are only open weekends*
so far out *that he makes the new math look like old stuff*
more factually *than it has been abroad*

No examples of structures like Nida's *here where the church stood* were found.

Table 19 shows the distribution of the various modifiers of adverb-heads. Adverbs represent nearly 50 per cent of the modifiers, and the distribution of nouns and noun sequences, clauses, and prepositional sequences appearing as modifiers is relatively even. For the first time, however, we find prepositional sequences trailing. Prepositional sequences represent no more than 25 per cent of the modifiers of adverb-heads in some categories and as little as one-seventh of the modifiers in other categories.

Table 20 shows the distribution between pre-posed and post-posed modifiers. Pre-posed modifiers, as the table indicates, are more common than post-posed modifiers of adverb-heads.

---

[18] *Synopsis*, p. 142.
[19] *Synopsis*, p. 142.

TABLE 19

Modification of adverbs in all newspapers in 1894 and in 1964

Modifiers	Complete Stories				Leads Only			
	1894		1964		1894		1964	
	No.	%	No.	%	No.	%	No.	%
Nouns and Noun Sequences	6	21.4	10	41.7	7	30.4	8	22.8
Adverbs	12	42.8	10	41.7	10	43.5	16	45.7
Clauses	6	21.4	2	3.2	—	—	4	14.3
Prepositional Sequences	4	14.3	2	3.2	6	26.1	6	17.1
total	28	99.9	24	100.0	23	100.1	35	99.9

TABLE 20

Distribution of modifiers of adverb-heads in all newspapers in 1894 and in 1964

Position	Complete Stories				Leads Only			
	1894		1964		1894		1964	
	No.	%	No.	%	No.	%	No.	%
Pre-adverb	15	53.6	18	75.0	17	74.0	22	62.8
Post-adverb	13	46.4	6	25.0	6	26.0	13	37.1
total	28	100.0	24	100.0	23	100.0	35	99.9

C. PREPOSITIONAL SEQUENCES AS HEADS

Prepositional sequences which appear so frequently as modifiers may also be the head of a structure of modification. This is not, as Table 21 shows, a frequent occurrence, but instances appear regularly.

Modifiers of prepositional sequences include nouns and noun sequences, adjectives, adverbs, and other prepositional sequences. Nida and Francis cite examples as follows:[20] nouns and noun sequences as modifiers of prepositional sequences:

Francis	*a bit* under the weather
	a mile off shore
	a long way off base
Nida	*a little* over 10
	a mile beyond the hill

[20] *American English*, p. 324; *Synopsis*, pp. 212—13.

TABLE 21

Modification of prepositional sequences in all newspapers in 1894 and in 1964

Modifier	Complete Stories				Leads Only			
	1894		1964		1894		1964	
	No.	%	No.	%	No.	%	No.	%
Nouns and Noun Sequences	1	7.1	—	—	14	51.8	8	42.1
Adjectives	1	7.1	—	—	1	3.7	—	—
Adverbs	12	85.7	11	78.6	9	33.3	11	57.9
Prepositional Sequences	—	—	3	21.4	3	11.1	—	—
total	14	99.9	14	100.0	27	99.9	19	100.0

Nouns and noun sequences as modifiers of prepositional sequences appear both pre-posed and post-posed in the materials examined in this study:

> *$84,064.09* in arrears
> *minutes* before death
> *this time* for a letter to the editor
> *a little* at sea
> *six months* after the slaying
> *$13 million* below expectations
>
> at the American premier *tomorrow night*
> at the Columbus theater *last night*
> from the same period *last year*
> during the annual winter discontent *the past few weeks*

Francis cites one example of an adverb as a post-posed modifier of a prepositional sequences:[21]

> on the mark *exactly*

In the materials examined in this study a number of adverbs appeared as post-posed modifiers of prepositional sequences:

> for some time *now*
> from 2 to 5 p.m. *daily*
> until sundown *yesterday*

[21] *American English*, p. 324.

Neither Nida or Francis cite any examples of adjectives as modifiers of prepositional sequences, but one example appeared in the materials examined in this study:

fresh *from the hands of the builders*

Prepositional sequences may also modify prepositional sequences, although this is a less common occurrence than other types of modification. Nida and Francis cite no examples, but the following examples appeared in the materials examined in this study:

at 1 a.m. *on Saturday*
at the opening *in Philadelphia*
in his sermon *in the Bloomingdale church*

Table 21 shows the distribution of the various modifiers of prepositional sequences and Table 22 shows the distribution of the modifiers in relation to the head.

TABLE 22

Distribution of modifiers of prepositional sequences in all newspapers in 1894 and in 1964

Position	Complete Stories				Leads Only			
	1894		1964		1894		1964	
	No.	%	No.	%	No.	%	No.	%
Pre-posed	9	64.3	11	78.6	12	44.4	13	68.4
Post-posed	5	35.7	3	21.4	15	55.6	6	31.6
total	14	100.0	14	100.0	27	100.0	19	100.0

D. NOUN DETERMINERS AS HEADS

Noun markers or determiners, Fries' Group A function words, may appear as heads in structures of modification. They may have both pre-posed and post-posed modifiers, but modification is limited and not frequent. Only nouns, adverbs and propositional sequences appear as modifiers of noun markers in the materials examined in this study, as Table 23 shows.

TABLE 23

Modification of noun markers (determiners) in all newspapers in 1894 and in 1964

Modifiers	Complete Stories				Leads Only			
	1894		1964		1894		1964	
	No.	%	No.	%	No.	%	No.	%
Nouns	13	50.0	3	17.6	9	25.0	—	—
Adverbs	9	34.6	8	47.1	25	69.4	9	69.2
Prepositional Sequences	4	15.4	6	35.3	2	5.6	4	30.8
total	26	100.0	17	100.0	36	100.0	13	100.0

Francis cites the examples below as typical of marker-headed structures of modification.[22] He limits modifiers to adverbs, qualifiers, and prepositional sequences, but some of his qualifiers are adverbs and one is a noun.[23] His examples:

adverbs

> *very* many people
> *not* a few friends

function noun

> *much* more money

prepositional sequence

> more *than enough* money

Nida cites examples of pre-posed modifiers of noun determiners, but no examples of post-posed modifiers. His examples:[24]

adverbs

> *nearly* a pint
> *not* a man
> *just* these two
> *such* a man

function nouns

> *both* the people

[22] *American English*, p. 324.
[23] See *American English*, p. 279: *rather, somewhat, still, much* are adverbs; *a little, a lot, a bit, lots, a good deal, a mite* are nouns and noun sequences.
[24] *Synopsis*, pp. 82—83.

Nida gives no other examples of usage, but cites a lengthy list of pre-determiner modifiers, including a number of adverbs with the derivational affix *-ly*; the adverbs *about, twice, also*; the function nouns *many, all, what* and *half*; and the prepositional sequence *at least*.[25]

In the materials examined in this study, the examples below appeared in pre-determiner position:

nouns and function nouns

> *number* 7
> *25 times* more
> *a little* more than one third
> *half* the city's school population
> *all* the union men
> *many* a day

adverbs

> *about* 4
> *almost* 5
> *just* 7
> *nearly* 4
> *not* less than 15,000
> *scarcely* any
> *so* much
> *as* many
> *but* two
> *possibly* 5
> *approximately* 125,000
> *fully* 15,000
> *not* a member
> *such* a long trip
> *only* the toleration
> *almost* a year
> *often* the object of criticism
> *about* a mile
> *earlier* this month

prepositional sequence

> *at least* two police officers
> *at least* eight centuries old

We have two types of modification here: (1) pre-posed modifiers of the determiner; and (2) pre-posed modifiers of a sequence consisting of a determiner

---

[25] *Synopsis*, p. 82.

and noun or noun sequence. In the following examples, the determiner is the head:

> *a little* more
> *25 times* more
> *fully* 15,000
> *at least* two police officers

In the following examples the whole sequence is the head of the structure of modification:

> *earlier* this month
> *all* the union men
> *many* a day
> *half* the city's school population
> *often* the object of criticism

Where the determiner is also a function noun, the pre-posed modifier stands in modifier relationship only to the determiner:

> *only* 3
> *possibly* 5

Where the determiner is a definite or indefinite article, a personal pronoun or a specifier, the pre-posed modifier stands in modifier relationship to the entire sequence:

> *many* a day
> *all* the union men
> *earlier* this month
> *half* her salary

Where the modifier is post-posed to the determiner, the modifier stands in modifier relationship only to the determiner. Of course, the whole sequence of determiner and modifier or modifiers then stands in modifier relationship to the noun which the determiner marks. Post-posed modifiers of determiners are limited to prepositional sequences and adverbs:

> more *than social*
> less *than happy*
> more *than 500 million*
> as many *as 50*
> one *more*

Table 23 shows the distribution of noun determiners in all four newspapers in the two years under study and in lead sentences and representative sentences. As the table indicates, there appears to be a lessening of the use of nouns and adverbs as modifiers of determiners and an increase in the use of prepositional sequences. However, the occurrence of this type of modification is so limited that the figures are not particularly significant. Table 24 shows the distribution of pre-posed modifiers and post-posed modifiers. Pre-posed modifiers outnumber by far the post-posed modifiers.

TABLE 24

Distribution of modifiers of noun markers (determiners) in all newspapers in 1894 and in 1964

Position	Complete Stories				Leads Only			
	1894		1964		1894		1964	
	No.	%	No.	%	No.	%	No.	%
Pre-determiner	22	84.6	11	64.7	32	88.9	10	76.9
Post-determiner	4	15.4	6	35.3	4	11.1	3	23.1
total	26	100.0	17	100.0	36	100.0	13	100.0

E. SENTENCES AND CLAUSES AS HEADS

So far we have examined structures of modification in which nouns, verbs, adjectives, adverbs, noun markers, prepositional sequences, and noun sequences were the heads. Sentences may also be the head of a structure of modification, and it is to the sentence-headed structure of modification to which we now turn.

Sentence-headed structures of modification consist of a sentence and various modifiers which may be pre-posed, occur within the sentence, or be post-posed to the sentence. Modifiers of sentence-heads include nouns and noun sequences, adjectives, adverbs, verbs, clauses, prepositional sequences, and a modifier which we find in use nowhere else — the ABSOLUTE CONSTRUCTION. The frequency and distribution of these various modifiers is shown in Table 25.

The sentence-head in most cases consists of one of the sentence types described by Fries in which there is a contrast between a class 1 word (a noun) and a Form Class 2 word (a verb).[26] This is the subject + predicate relationship of the normal English sentence. However, in a written corpus such as the one used in this study, other independent structures appear which do not show this contrast. These may be structures like the response, call, or exclama-

TABLE 25

Modification of sentences in all newspapers in 1894 and in 1964

Modifiers	Complete Stories				Leads Only			
	1894		1964		1894		1964	
	No.	%	No.	%	No.	%	No.	%
Nouns and Noun								
Sequences	1	1.3	2	4.5	1	1.7	1	3.3
Adjectives	1	1.3	1	2.3	1	1.7	—	—
Adverbs	15	20.0	8	18.2	—	—	1	3.3
Verbs								
present part	7	9.3	5	11.4	4	6.8	4	13.3
past part	—	—	—	—	—	—	1	3.3
infinitives	1	1.3	—	—	1	1.7	1	3.3
total	8	10.6	5	11.4	5	8.5	6	20.0
Clauses	15	20.0	8	18.2	19	32.2	10	33.3
Prepositional								
Sequences	35	46.7	20	45.5	27	45.8	11	36.7
Absolute								
Constructions	—	—	—	—	6	10.2	1	3.3
total	75	99.9	4	100.1	59	100.1	30	99.8

tion sentences described by Francis.[27] Most of the sentences which appear as heads of structures of modification, however, will be structures consisting of a subject + predicate and the various modifiers associated with the two.

Modifiers of sentences, as it has already been noted, may appear in one of three positions: pre-posed to the head; within the sentence-head; and post-posed to the sentence-head. This distribution is shown in Table 26.

TABLE 26

Distribution of modifiers of sentences in all newspapers in 1894 and in 1964

Position	Complete Stories				Leads Only			
	1894		1964		1894		1964	
	No.	%	No.	%	No.	%	No.	%
Pre-sentence	48	64.0	32	72.7	30	50.8	17	56.7
Within	10	13.3	4	9.1	8	13.5	—	—
Post-sentence	17	22.7	8	18.2	21	35.6	13	43.3
total	75	100.0	44	100.0	59	99.9	30	100.0

[26] *Structure*, pp. 144—45 and ff.
[27] *American English*, pp. 374—389.

1. Pre-posed Modifiers

Pre-posed modifiers are most common and represent 50 per cent or more of the sentence-modifiers in every instance. There are fewer post-posed modifiers, and the appearance of modifiers within the sentence-head, usually between the subject and the predicate, is least common of all as Table 26 shows.

Examples of the various types of sentence-modifiers are given below. Included are clauses as sentence-modifiers, as cited by Francis and Nida:[28]

Francis   *When he comes*, we will go.
               If it rains, close the window.

Nida   They will never get it right, *which after all will be to our advantage somewhat*.
               I told them I thought so too, *which didn't make the slightest difference to them*.

Prepositional sequences as sentence-modifiers, as cited by Francis and Nida:[29]

Francis   He is innocent, *in my opinion*.
               At the corner, a policeman was directing traffic.

Nida   *On the contrary*, I believe . . .
               In consequence, do you believe . . .

Verbs as sentence-modifiers as cited by Francis and Nida include both present participles and infinitives.[30] Past participles may also serve as sentence-modifiers, but none were cited by Francis or Nida. Their examples:

Francis   *To be sure*, he didn't mean it.
               To drive well, you must always be alert.
               Continuing our story, the next chapter is a sad one.

Nida   *To tell the truth*, this is not . . .
               To be honest, this thing is too shaken to . . .

Adverbs as sentence-modifiers, as cited by Francis and Nida:[31]

Francis   *Obviously*, he was lying.
               Naturally, I am opposed to war.

---

[28] *American English*, p. 400; *Synopsis*, p. 188.
[29] *American English*, p. 403; *Synopsis*, p. 187.
[30] *American English*, pp. 401—402; *Synopsis*, p. 188.
[31] *American English*, p. 403; *Synopsis*, pp. 186—87.

Nida   *Undoubtedly*, this proposition will mean a great deal.
              Altogether, this is most unfortunate.

Nida cites the following examples of nouns or noun sequences as sentence-modifiers:[32]

Nida   *Sympathy or no sympathy*, I wanted to go . . .
              All the same, this is going . . .

Nida also cites what he refers to as parenthetical expressions and which Francis calls clauses with a zero includer.[33] These are expressions like *I thought, I think, I suppose*, which appear within a sentence or post-posed. The examples which appeared in the materials examined in this study were lumped with other clauses.

Absolute constructions are the only modifiers which have not appeared as modifiers of other types of heads. No examples are cited by Nida, but Francis gives the following illustrations:[34]

Francis   *the vans having arrived*, we were ready to move
                 work finished, we went home
                 the rain over, we went indoors
                 Stalin dead, the way was clear for Malenkov

Francis defines these absolute constructions as noun-headed structures of modification with a post-posed modifier consisting of a participle, either present or past, and sometimes other modifiers, as in his example, *the rain over*.[35]

PRE-POSED MODIFIERS

In the materials examined in this study, the following examples of pre-posed modifiers of sentence-heads were found:

(Nouns and noun sequences)

> *The next morning*, they decided to drive right on through to Sunnyvale — the men taking turns at the wheel.
> *Just two months before the opening of the New York World's Fair, on April 23*, the Fair is a fanciful never-never land firmly grounded in no-nonsense mud.

---

[32] *Synopsis*, p. 187.
[33] *American English*, p. 404; *Synopsis*, p. 189.
[34] *American English*, pp. 400—401.
[35] *American English*, p. 401.

(adjective)

> And, *third*, Mr. Kennedy saw the need to provide an adequate space program.

(adverbs)

> *Fourteen years ago*, Mr. Beckman and his wife, the former Jeanne Jacoby took part in the inauguration in Israel of the Techneon's 300-acre campus.
> *Two years later*, he was named Acting Queen's County Judge in the Appellate Division of the Supreme Court and remained in that post until becoming fire commissioner.

(verbs)

> *Reversing himself with a suddenness that caught many civil rights leaders by surprise*, the Rev. Milton A Galamison announced yesterday that a second school boycott would be held here on March 6.

(clauses)

> *When you want a thin idea spun out into an attenuated play*, apply to Keith Waterhouse and Willis Hall.
> *If Frank Charles Carlucci 3rd, the new United States chargé d'affaires in Zanzibar, finds things a bit difficult in his new post*, it will be no new experience.

(prepositional sequences)

> *Since 1949* the service has pursued an anti-discrimination policy, Bernstein said.
> *At his Yerba Buena home*, he was serenaded by school children.

(absolute construction)

> *His dander up*, Governor Rockefeller lashed out yesterday at American "secrecy" in Viet Nam and took sharp issue with President Johnson's suggestion that foreign policy is a sacred cow as far as politics is concerned.

2. Modifiers Within the Head

As Table 26 shows, there are fewer instances of modification of sentence-heads where the modifier is is placed within the head. A few examples from the materials examined for this study:

(adverbs)

> Mr. Davis, *therefore*, had to refuse to accept the bail.
> The concessionaires, *too*, are deserving of praise for their courtesy to the children.

(clauses)

> Mr. Healy, *when seen by a reporter for the New York Times*, admitted that the appointment was a surprise.
>
> Abraham Reimer, nine–years–old, of No. 47 Morrell st., Williamsburg, was run over and, *it is thought*, fatally injured by trolley car No. 1,913 of the Graham ave. line, yesterday afternoon.

(prepositional sequence)

> It was hit, *for instance*, for $1,050 last May; $900 in March of 1962; twice in 1961 for $1,000 and $1,975; and for $624 in 1958.
>
> Erastus Wiman, *through his counsel, Gen. Benjamin F. Tracy, in the Court of General Sessions, before Judge Martine*, yesterday pleaded not guilty to two indictments found against him last week for forgery in the second degree.

3. Post-Posed Modifiers

In the materials examined for this study, as Table 26 shows, a limited number of instances of post-posed modifiers of sentence-heads occurred. Some example:

(verbs)

> An explosion shattered a storage room in the Chicago stadium, 1800 Madison st., late yesterday afternoon, *injuring Robert Horton, 32, of 6117 May st., a porter*.
>
> The June 2 primary election in California will be crucial for Goldwater and Rockefeller, Nixon said, *terming it "a sudden-death play-off in which both of them will be toe-to-toe, slugging it out."*

(clauses)

> The executive board of the Chicago Teachers union voted unanimously to postpone a strike vote yesterday, *after the board of education approved a "collective bargaining memorandum" with the union*.
>
> Nikolai Okhlopkov, a leading theatrical director of the Soviet Union, is not coming to the United States, *although, the State Department and the Soviet Ministry of Culture had approved the six-week visit*.

(prepositional sequences)

> Four men exposed to severe radiation in an accident at Oak Ridge, Tenn., in 1958, seem to have recovered from radiation-caused sterility, *according to a report published yesterday*.

(absolute constructions)

> The Roby bookmakers had a breathing spell yesterday, *but two favorites winning*.

> The course of yesterday's wheat market was gratifying to the bulls, *the price selling up 1½ cents for Wednesday's official close and holding much of the advance.*

The structure we have defined as a sentence-head appears not only alone as an independent linguistic form, but it appears quite frequently as one of the structures making a larger independent linguistic form. These larger independent linguistic structures may consist of two sentences linked by conjunctions, *and, but,* or *or,* for example. Francis defines these as compound sentences:[36]

> The spring has come, *but* the weather is cold.

In other instances, the sentence is used as modifier of a noun, verb or other head, including sentence-heads, by means of a linkage provided by words like *because, after, since, although, who, which, that* or zero, words which are frequently referred to as includers[31] Sentences thus brought into other structures by means of includers have already been identified as *included clauses.*

As we have already seen, included clauses appear as modifiers of nouns, verbs and other words and as modifiers of sentences:

> news *that the war is over*
> came *after I left*
> stronger *than he was before*
> *when he comes,* we will go

The point to be stressed here is that included clauses and sentences are basically the same structure and both show the same characteristic contrast between noun and verb described by Fries in his discussion of sentence types. The sentence and the clause, essentially the same linguistic structure, are modified in essentially the same way. As Tables 22 and 28 show, sentence-modifiers are also clause modifiers and they appear in the same characteristic positions.

Since both clauses and sentences are modified in the same way and by the same modifiers, there is no reason to cite further examples of the modifiers from Nida, Francis, or the newspapers examined. Comparison of Tables 25 and 27 show that there is considerably less modification of clauses than of sentences and that the frequence with which certain modifiers appear is somewhat different. Comparison of Tables 26 and 28 show somewhat the same pattern of distribution for modifiers of sentences and modifiers of clauses

---

[36] *American English,* pp. 415—16.
[37] *American English,* p. 389. *ff.*

TABLE 27

Modification of clauses in all newspapers in 1894 and in 1964

| Modifier | Complete Stories | | | | Leads Only | | | |
| | 1894 | | 1964 | | 1894 | | 1964 | |
	No.	%	No.	%	No.	%	No.	%
Nouns	1	3.3	1	16.7	—	—	1	7.1
Noun Sequences	2	6.7	—	—	3	12.5	—	—
total	3	10.0	1	16.7	3	12.5	1	7.1
Adverbs	4	13.3	1	16.7	4	16.7	5	35.7
Verbs								
present part	3	10.0	—	—	3	12.5	1	7.1
past part	—	—	—	—	1	4.2	—	—
infinitives	—	—	—	—	—	—	—	—
total	3	10.0	—	—	4	16.7	1	7.1
Clauses	11	36.7	2	333.	2	8.3	5	35.7
Prepositional								
Sequences	9	30.0	2	33.3	11	45.8	2	14.3
total	30	100.0	6	100.0	24	100.0	14	99.9

TABLE 28

Distribution of modifiers of clauses in all newspapers in 1894 and in 1964

| Position | Complete Stories | | | | Leads Only | | | |
| | 1894 | | 1964 | | 1894 | | 1964 | |
	No.	%	No.	%	No.	%	No.	%
Pre-clause	21	70.0	6	100.0	20	83.3	10	71.4
Within	2	6.7	—	—	—	—	2	14.3
Post-clause	7	23.3	—	—	4	16.7	2	14.3
total	30	100.0	6	100.0	24	100.0	14	100.0

Information contained in Tables 27 and 28 and in Tables 25 and 26 is combined in Tables 29 and 30 below. These combined tables show that again the prepositional sequence is the most frequent modifier and that the clause represents the second largest group of sentence or clause modifiers. The tables show some differences between the modification in lead sentences and in representative sentences, and show also that in lead sentences there has been a shift in the distribution of modifiers from 1894 to 1964. While the distribution in representative sentences remained very nearly the same over the 70-year period, the distribution in lead sentences shifted. Fewer prepositional sequences appeared as sentence and clause modifiers in 1964, but clauses and adverbs increased as sentence and clause modifiers. Verbs as modifiers increased slightly.

It is interesting to note that the absolute constructions are infrequent and that they appeared only in lead sentences. Adjectives appeared too infrequently to be significant, and nouns and noun sequences, also relatively few, seemed stable.

TABLE 29

Modification of sentences and clauses in all newspapers in 1894 and in 1964

Modifiers	Complete Stories				Leads Only			
	1894		1964		1894		1964	
	No.	%	No.	%	No.	%	No.	%
Nouns	1	1.0	—	—	—	—	1	2.3
Noun Sequences	3	2.8	2	4.1	4	4.8	1	2.3
total	4	3.8	2	4.1	4	4.8	2	4.5
Adjectives	1	1.1	1	2.0	1	1.2	—	—
Adverbs	19	18.1	9	18.4	4	4.8	6	13.6
Verbs								
present part	10	9.5	5	10.2	7	8.4	5	11.4
past part	—	—	—	—	1	1.2	1	2.3
infinitives	1	1.0	—	—	1	1.2	1	2.3
total	11	10.5	5	10.2	9	10.8	7	16.0
Clauses	26	24.8	10	20.4	21	25.3	15	34.1
Prepositional Sequences	44	42.0	22	44.9	38	45.8	13	29.5
Absolute Constructions	—	—	—	—	6	7.2	1	2.3
total	105	100.2	49	100.0	83	99.9	44	100.0

TABLE 30

Distribution of modifiers of sentences and clauses in all newspapers in 1894 and in 1964

Position	Complete Stories				Leads Only			
	1894		1964		1894		1964	
	No.	%	No.	%	No.	%	No.	%
Pre-posed	69	65.7	37	75.5	50	60.2	27	61.4
Within	12	11.4	4	8.2	8	9.6	2	4.5
Post-posed	24	22.9	8	16.3	25	30.1	15	34.1
total	105	100.0	49	100.0	83	99.9	44	100.0

VII

CONCLUSIONS:
THE SYSTEM OF MODIFICATION

The system of modification in present-day American English, as seen in this study, is a formal and intricate system; it is a highly predictable system, and, in practice, paradoxically, an amazingly simple system.

The system of modification might be called intricate because it consists of carefully built up layers. Single words and larger structures, including the sentence, can be modified, and their modifiers can be modified — and THEIR modifiers can be modified — and so on. A single word, for example, may be modified by a sentence — a structure that itself may contain single word modifiers and structures of modification serving as modifiers.

DeMorgan's great fleas with little fleas upon their backs is a counterpart of the system of modification in which modifiers can be modified, and these modifiers in turn be modified, and so on *ad infinitum.*

A. AN INTRICATE SYSTEM

Intricacy of the system can be demonstrated by a basic sentence like the following, in which the parentheses indicate positions where the modifiers of the noun-subject and noun-object, in italics, can be placed:

> The ( ) contract ( ) was a ( ) package ( )
> The ( ) contract *that settled the ( ) dispute* ( ) was a ( ) package ( )
> The ( ) contract that settled the ( ) dispute ( ) was a *$36 million* package ( )
> The ( ) contract that settled the ( ) dispute ( ) was a $36 million package *that went into ( ) effect ( )*
> The ( ) contract that settled the ( ) dispute ( ) was a $36 million package that went into ( ) effect *in ( ) June ( )*

Although this sentence, taken from the materials examined for this study, is now complete, there are still six positions that could be filled with modifiers of nouns. Other modifying positions are present, of course, but they have not been indicated.

Another example, this time showing the modification possible when the original head-word is a single-word noun-subject:

> *One* was a(n) admiral
> One ( )
> One *of the* ( ) *golfers* ( )
> One of the *keen-eyed golfers who played* ( )

Addition of modifiers of the noun-subject began with a post-posed prepositional sequence. Next the noun *golfers* was modified by an included clause whose verb can now be modified, and by an adjective which, too, can be modified.

> One of the *most* keen-eyed golfers who played *at the* ( ) *Country Club* ( )
> One of the most keen-eyed golfers who played at the *Army-Navy* Country Club ( )
> One of the most keen-eyed golfers who played at the Army-Navy Country Club *outside Washington* ( )
> One of the most-keen-eyed golfers who played at the Army-Navy Country Club outside Washington *a few years ago* ( )

This structure of modification, starting with a single noun-subject, now includes 20 words and these modifiers:

> three prepositional sequences
> one included clause
> one adjective
> one adverb-headed structure of modification
> one adverb
> one noun-headed structure of modification
> one structure of coordination

The original noun-head, one, is modified by a single modifier, the prepositional sequence *of the golfers*. All the rest of the modification is built up within this sequence. The noun *golfers* is modified by two modifiers — first, an adjective-headed structure of modification consisting of an adjective-head, *keen-eyed*, and an adverb-modifier, *most;* second, by an included clause introduced by *who*. This included clause contains the verb *played* which is modified by two prepositional sequences, *at the Country Club* and *outside Washington*, and an adverb-headed structure of modification, *a few years ago*. The adverb *ago* is modified by a pre-posed modifier consisting of a noun-headed structure of modification, *a few years*. This last structure consists of a noun-head modified by the adjective *few* and a noun marker. In one of the prepositional sequences modifying *played*, *at the Country Club*, the noun sequence *Country Club* is modified by a structure of coordination consisting of two nouns *Army-Navy*.

Let us look at another example of this intricate, layer upon layer building up of a sequence through modification. In this example, the verb and its modifiers are expanded through further modification:

> The question was put ( )
> The question was put *to him* ( )
> The question was put to him *as he arrived* ( )
> The question was put to him as he arrived *under an assumed name* ( )
> The question was put to him as he arrived under an assumed name
>   *after a flight* ( )
> The question was put to him as he arrived under an assumed name
>   after a flight *from San Juan* ( )

In this example, the verb *was put* has been modified by the prepositional sequence *to him*. The verb and its modifier — *was put to him* — is modified by the clause *as he arrived*. The clause contains, a verb, *arrived*, which is modified by two prepositional sequences, *under an assumed name*, and *after a flight*. The noun *flight* in the last sequence is modified by another prepositional sequence, *from San Juan*.

Only a few of the modifying positions possible in this sentence have actually been filled. For example:

> ( ) question ( )
> ( ) was ( ) put ( )
> an ( ) assumed name ( )
> a ( ) flight from ( ) San Juan ( )

B. A PREDICTABLE SYSTEM

In addition to its intricacy, the system of modification in present-day American English has a high degree of predictability based, first, on the regular, fixed positions of modifiers, and, second, on the regularity with which certain modifiers appear in these positions.

All single words which can be modified, and all the larger structures — sequences, sentences, and clauses — may be modified by pre-posed and post-posed modifiers, thus:

( ) NOUN ( )
( ) ADJECTIVE ( )
( ) ADVERB ( )
( ) NOUN MARKER ( )

Some sequences, the verb sequence consisting of an auxiliary verb and a main verb, the clause, and the sentence, have a third position within the sequence:

verb sequence
    ( ) auxiliary ( ) main verb ( )
clause
    includer ( ) subject ( ) predicate ( )
sentence
    ( ) subject ( ) predicate ( )

Not all these available positions are always filled, of course, but they may be and in the case of nouns and verbs extensive use is made of these modifying positions as Table 31 and earlier tables show.

TABLE 31

A comparison of the frequency of modification of the various heads in structures of modification analyzed in this study

| Heads | Complete Stories | | | | Leads Only | | | |
| | 1894 | | 1964 | | 1894 | | 1964 | |
	No.	%	No.	%	No.	%	No.	%
Nouns								
pre-posed	949	36.3	1276	44.0	1411	40.5	1617	44.8
post-posed	700	26.8	756	26.1	984	28.7	907	25.1
total	1649	63.1	2032	70.1	2395	68.7	2524	69.9
Verbs								
alone	467	17.9	472	16.3	575	16.4	591	16.4
+ comp. or obj.	178	6.8	205	7.1	237	6.1	295	8.2
total	645	24.8	677	23.3	812	22.5	886	24.6
Sentences	75	2.3	44	1.5	59	1.7	30	.8
Clauses	30	1.2	6	.2	24	.7	14	.4
total	105	4.1	50	1.7	83	2.4	44	1.2
Adjectives	41	1.7	35	1.2	52	1.5	44	1.2
Adverbs	28	1.0	24	.8	23	.7	35	.9
Markers	26	1.0	17	.6	36	1.0	13	.4
Prepositional								
Sequences	14	.6	14	.5	27	.8	19	.5
total	2613	99.9	2899	99.9	3475	100.0	3609	99.9

Tables accompanying the discussion of the various structures of modification show which of the possible modifier positions are most often used. In the verb-headed structures of modification, for example, from 65 to 70 per cent of the modifiers are post-posed to the verb; another 27 to 33 per cent appear after the verb and its object or subjective complement; 10 per cent or fewer of the modifiers appear pre-posed or between the auxiliary verb and the main verb.[1] In noun-headed structures of modification, the ratio is about 5 to 3 between pre-nominal and post-nominal modifiers.[2]

A quantitative study like the present one makes it possible to predict with some certainty not only which of the fixed, modifying positions will be filled most frequently, but what modifiers are most likely to occupy these positions. In noun-headed structures of modification, for example, in the pre-nominal position, the following modifiers appear in these ratios:[3]

(the) _____ NOUN + _____

        nouns (50 to 55 per cent)
            publicity
            Pentagon
            standard

        adjectives (35 to 50 per cent)
            good
            able
            friendly

        verbs (less than 2 per cent)
            following
            murdered

        adverbs (less than 1 per cent)
            then
            late

In the post-nominal modifying position, the following modifiers appear in these ratios:

        prepositional sequences   (60 to 65 per cent)
            of the hour
            in all good time
            from New York

[1] See Table 10.
[2] See Tables 1 and 8.
[3] See Tables 1 and 8.

nouns and noun sequences (about 20 per cent)

> the expert
> the same size
> president

verbs (6 to 8 per cent)

> devoted to his family
> to be feared

adjectives (1 to 2 per cent)

> general
> martial

adverbs (about 1 per cent)

> today
> here

The percentages given above are approximations of the percentages for both 1894 and 1964 and for both representative and lead sentences. More exact figures are given in the tables in the previous chapters.

C. A SIMPLE SYSTEM

The intricacy of the system of modification, as we have seen, lies partly in the fact that there are so many possible positions for modifiers even in a brief sequence, and partly in the fact that each modifier added to a sequence brings with it new positions subject to modification.

But despite this possibility for complexity — and occasional actual complexity — the system of modification is basically simple, and for one good reason: the system is never overloaded. First, not all possible modifying positions are used in any given situation, and, second, only a minimum of modifiers appear with any one head-word.

If we refer to Table 3, for example, we see that in 75 per cent of all noun-headed structures of modification where the modifiers are pre-posed that the modifier is limited to a single word.[4] And Table 9 shows that where noun-heads have post-posed modifiers in 40 per cent of the instances the head has only a single post-posed modifier:[5]

> a friend *of the slain woman*
> two *of CORE's most militant branches*
> commander *of the fleet's sonar school*

[4] See Table 3.
[5] See Table 9.

In about 40 per cent of the instances of post-nominal modification, the noun-head has a single post-nominal modifier and one or more pre-nominal modifiers:

> a *unique* block *of four United States airmail stamps*
> a *sweeping* command *of rhythm*

Verb modification is even simpler, as Table 12 shows.[6] More than 50 per cent of the verb-heads have single modifiers; roughly 28 to 38 per cent have only two modifiers; 12 to 13 per cent have three modifiers, and only about $2\frac{1}{2}$ per cent have four modifiers. Less than 1 per cent of all verb-heads have more than four modifiers.

A single modifier, sometimes two modifiers for each head, is more common than more complex patterns. Frequently, too, when a single head has two modifiers, each will occupy a different position. There is very little piling up of modifiers in a single modifying position as Table 3 shows us concerning noun-head.[7]

Another factor in the simplicity of the system of modification is the fact that although words and sequences frequently change positions in a sentence, and change their function, they are always modified in the same way. Modification is consistent. It does not shift with position. For example, a noun may be a subject, direct object, indirect object, an objective complement, or the modifier of a verb, adjective clause, sentence, or another noun. But regardless of function or position, the noun is modified in exactly the same way:

Nouns in subject position, modified pre-nominally and post-nominally:

> The *Mexican* Ambassador *to Bolivia*
> *New* plans *for a municipal nursing home*

Nouns in object position, also pre-nominally and post-nominally modified:

> announce the date *of the second boycott*
> will accomplish *immediate* separation *from the department*
> has the *exclusively realistic and representational* art *of the Hartford collection*

Nouns in prepositional sequences, modified pre-nominally and post-nominally:

> for reasons *of health*
> for the *first* boycott
> for his *absorbing* lectures *on the humanities*

[6] See Table 12.
[7] See Table 3.

Nouns modifying other words or structures may themselves be modified. Here nouns modifying verbs are modified pre-nominally and post-nominally:

> sold *last* night
> arrived *early* Tuesday
> works seven days *a week*

Verbs, similarly, take their modifiers with them when they move from a verb position in the predicate to various modifying positions in the sentence. And form class words of one class which assume the position and positional characteristics of another form class retain their original idiosyncrasies of modification as long as they maintain their morphological identity. For example, adjectives like *brave, good, best, wisest*, sometimes appear in a noun-subject position in a sentence and are marked by position and by the presence of noun markers as nouns.

> The *good* die young.
> The *brave* deserve the victory.
> The *best* is yet to come.

Adjectives like these, in noun positions, functioning as subject of the sentence, and marked by the characteristic noun marker *the* might be called function nouns, nominals, noun substitutes or noun replacements, all terms hinting at a noun quality acquired by position, function, and marking by a noun marker.

However, these words still retain their morphological identity as adjectives and are modified like adjectives:

> the _____ brave
>   truly
>   really
>   very
>   quite

We see the same thing in sentences like the following where the adjective occupies what is sometimes considered the true noun-subject position and the filler *it* is in the usual noun-subject position:

> It is *certain*
> It seems *probable*.

Certain and probable are adjectives here and may be modified accordingly by adverbs such as *very, quite, most, absolutely* and others.

It is *quite certain*.
It seems *absolutely probable*.

However, if these adjectives are given noun suffixes, become nouns morphologically and thus become members of another form class, they take on a new character. They will be modified like nouns and lose their ability to appear with modifiers restricted to adjectives:

It is a _____ certainty.
          real
          absolute
          near
          clear

There is an overall simplicity, too, in the fact that the two most frequently employed modifiers, nouns and prepositional sequences, move freely from one position to another and can modify any head-word. It we add clauses, which modify anything except prepositional sequences and noun markers we have 70 per cent of all modifiers accounted for. Adjectives, adverbs, and verbs have a more restricted range and frequency. While any word or sequence can act as a modifier of another word or sequence — and will do so at some time — most modification is accomplished by nouns, prepositional sequences, and clauses, the most flexible of the modifiers.

TABLE 32

Summary of the various modifiers appearing with all head-words in all newspapers in 1894 and in 1964

Modifiers	Complete Stories				Leads Only			
	1894		1964		1894		1964	
	No.	%	No.	%	No.	%	No.	%
Nouns/Noun Sequences	678	27.1	1016	35.7	1076	31.3	1283	36.3
Adjectives	433	17.3	455	16.0	580	16.9	592	16.7
Adverbs	225	9.0	230	8.1	260	7.5	365	10.3
Verbs	103	4.1	123	4.3	114	3.3	118	3.3
Clauses	136	5.4	114	4.0	149	4.3	124	3.5
Prepositional Sequences	930	37.1	911	32.0	1243	36.3	1052	29.8
Absolutes	—	—	—	—	6	.4	1	.1
total	2505	100.0	2849	100.1	3428	100.0	3535	99.9

D. SUMMARIES

Table 32 presents a summary of the various types of modifiers appearing in the materials examined in this study. Nouns and noun sequences together with prepositional sequences represent about two-thirds of all modifiers used in the newspapers examined in both years. Adjectives represent only 16 to 17 per cent of all modifiers, and other modifiers are infrequently used. The whole system is remarkably stable over the seventy-year period from 1894 to 1964, but there has been a slight shift in usage which should be noted. In both representative and lead sentences, use of prepositional sequences declined somewhat and the use of nouns and noun sequences increased from 1894 to 1964. Where prepositional sequences were the principal modifiers in 1894 by 10 per cent margin in representative sentences and by a 5 per cent margin in lead sentences, in 1964 they trailed behind nouns and noun sequences in use.

Table 31 is interesting in comparison with Table 32. It shows that nouns are the most modified of all head-words, roughly 70 per cent of all modifiers appearing with noun-heads, and that verbs are the next in number of modifiers. Between 20 and 25 per cent of all modifiers appear with verb-heads. Other heads show remarkably little modification. Totals shown in Table 31 do not represent the total number of head-words, but rather the number of modifiers appearing with head-words of the various classes.

E. APPLICATIONS OF THIS STUDY

This study and further studies of the same type which make quantitative analyses of systems within the language should have some practical use in applied linguistics. For example, a knowledge of what modifiers are most frequently used in certain types of writing might be of considerable use in teaching composition skills to native speakers of English at various levels. And the most frequently used modifiers and types of structures of modification, singled out as they are in a study like the present one, would seem to show where the emphasis should be placed in teaching non-native speakers about the use of English.

Linguistics relies on usage to show what a language is like, and usage implies not only what is possible, but what is done, and how frequently. A quantitative study such as this gives a new dimension to grammar, a dimension lacking in catalogues like Nida's and summaries like that of Francis. As this study shows, while all kinds of modification are possible, certain patterns are most common. Applied linguistics would find it more useful to know what structures of modification are actually in use, and the extent of their use, than to know that in a language as flexible and accommodating as English almost anything is possible.

F. SUGGESTIONS FOR FURTHER STUDY

A number of other studies are possible as a sequel to this analysis of the structures of modification in present-day American English.

First of all, this study might well be replicated using another sample from selected newspapers. The newspapers used in this study were selected because they were considered to represent the best in journalistic writing style, and perhaps another study based on other newspapers, not necessarily the best, might yield different data. Second, the same type of analysis might be made of other types of written American English.

A standard corpus of edited present-day American English has been compiled at Brown University and would probable be ideal for this purpose.[8] This corpus consists of more than a million words from various sources. It is written and edited, not spoken, English and consists of some 500 samples of approximately 2,000 words each, and includes some materials from newspapers, magazines, journals and various types of books, both fiction and non-fiction. This corpus is available on computer tape and no doubt an analysis similar to this, but using several different and larger samples, might be done by computer.

Other analyses might be suggested. Since prepositional sequences prove so great a part of the system of modification, further study of the system of prepositions might be worthwhile. What prepositions are most used or least used? Could a list be made of all prepositions in use and a relative value given to each? There would be some interest, too, in closer study of the adverb, particularly base adverbs which seem to have a number of functions and to appear in various positions in the sentence.

---

[8] See W. Nelson Francis, "A Standard Corpus of Edited Present-Day American English", *College English* XXVI (January, 1965), 267—273, for a description of the corpus. Several studies making use of the corpus have already been completed.

SELECTED BIBLIOGRAPHY

1. BOOKS

Bloomfield, Leonard, *Language* (New York, 1933, reprinted 1962).
Curme, George, O., *A Grammar of the English Language*. Vol. III, *Syntax* (New York, 1931).
Francis, W. Nelson, *The Structure of American English* (New York, 1958).
Fries, Charles Carpenter, *The Structure of English: An Introduction to the Construction of English Sentences* (New York and Burlingame, 1961).
Hill, A. A., *Introduction to Linguistic Structures* (New York, 1958).
Hockett, Charles F., *A Course in Modern Linguistics* (New York, 1958).
Nida, Eugene, *A Synopsis of English Syntax* (Norman, Okla., 1960, reprinted 1962).
Robertson, Stuart, *The Development of Modern English*, revised by Frederic G. Cassidy (Englewood Cliffs, N. J., 1954).
Strang, Barbara, *Modern English Structure* (New York, 1962).
Trager, George L and Henry Lee Smith, *An Outline of English Structure* (Washington, D. C., 1957).
Whitehall, Harold, *Structural Essentials of English* (New York, 1956).

2. ARTICLES

Francis, W. Nelson, "A Standard Corpus of Edited Present-Day American English", *College English*, XXVI (1965), 267—273.
Haugen, Einar "On Reading the Close Appositive", *American Speech*, XXVIII (1953), 165—170.

INDEX

absolute construction, 104
    as modifier of sentence head, 104, 105, 106, 107
adjectives
    as head in structure of modification, 86
    identification, 24—25
    as modifier of noun heads, 31—32
    as modifier of prepositional sequences, 97
    as modifier of sentences, 105
    as modifier of verb heads, 75, 78, 79
    with noun markers, table, 59
    as post-nominal modifiers, 61—62
    as pre-nominal modifiers, 31—32
adjective-headed structures of modification, 86
    adverbs as modifiers, 86—87; 90—91
    clauses as modifiers, 90
    modifiers in adjective-headed structures of modification, table, 86
    nouns as modifiers, 87, 88
    participial as post-posed modifier, 89
    position of modifiers, table, 92
    post-posed modifiers, 88—89
    pre-posed modifiers, 90
    prepositional sequences as modifiers, 89
adverbs
    conditioners or markers with adjective-headed structures of modification, 90
    head in structure of modification, 92
    identification, 25—27
    modifiers of adverb heads, 92
    modifiers of noun markers, 99
    modifiers of prepositional sequences, 96
    modifiers of sentences, 103, 105
    modifiers of verb heads, 75, 78, 79
    modifiers of verb + object heads, 82
    with noun markers, table 59

post-nominal modifiers, 62—63
pre-nominal modifiers, 45—46
adverb-headed structures of modification, 92
    adverbs as modifiers, 92
    clauses as modifiers, 94
    modifiers, table, 95
    nouns as modifiers, 93
    noun sequences as modifiers, 93
    position of modifiers, table, 95
    post-posed modifers, 93
    prepositional sequences as modifiers, 93
appositives, 36—44
    as post-nominal modifiers, 66
    titles as appositives, 38—39
    types, 43

clauses
    included clauses defined, 64, 107
    as modifier of adjective head, 90
    as modifier of adverb head, 94
    as modifier of sentence, 103, 105, 106
    as modifier of verb head, 76, 78, 79
    as modifier of verb + object head, 82
    as post-nominal modifier, 64—66
clause as head
    modification discussed, 107
    modifiers, table, 108, 109
    modifiers, distribution of, table, 108, 109
constructs (see sequences)
coordinate sequence
    as post-nominal modifier in noun-headed structures of modification, 50
corpus, composition of, 15—17

determiners (see noun markers)

JANUA LINGUARUM

STUDIA MEMORIAE NICOLAI VAN WIJK DEDICATA

Edited by C. H. van Schooneveld

SERIES PRACTICA

Some titles:

MOUTON · PUBLISHERS · THE HAGUE

6450 0402